Vintage Cars
IN COLOR

Introduction and commentaries by
Anthony Harding

Hippocrene Books, New York

Text Copyright © B. T. Batsford Ltd

ALL RIGHTS RESERVED

For information write to:
HIPPOCRENE BOOKS, INC.
171 Madison Avenue, New York, N.Y. 10016

Library of Congress Catalog Card Number 74-28798
ISBN 0-88254-323-7

Printed in Great Britain

Contents

Author's Note   4
Introduction   5

1920 Rolls-Royce 'Silver Ghost'   16
1920 Rover Eight   18
1920 Stanley 735-A   20
1921 Citroën Type A 10CV   22
1921 A.C. 11.9 h.p.   24
1923 Austin Seven   26
1923 37.2 h.p. Hispano-Suiza H6B   28
1924 Morris 'Cowley'   30
1924 Vauxhall 30/98   32
1925 Ford Model T   34
1925 Rolls-Royce 'Phantom I'   36
1925 Frazer Nash 1½-litre   38
1926 Bentley 3-litre Speed Model   40
1926 Alvis 12/50   42
1926 Sunbeam 3-litre   44
1927 Jowett 'Long Four'   46
1927 Isotta Fraschini Tipo 8A   48
1928 Bugatti Type 44   50
1928–29 Alfa Romeo 6C 1500   52
1928 Lancia Lambda (Eighth Series)   54
1929 38/250 Mercedes-Benz SSK   56
1929 Duesenberg Model J   58
1929 Irving-Napier 'Golden Arrow'   60
1930 M.G. 18/80 Mark II   62

Author's Note

'There is no historical fact about motoring history that cannot be proved wrong.' – Sam Clutton

No doubt industrious and erudite reviewers will pick many nits from the corpus of the text. However, as all the facts therein have been cribbed most carefully from the writings of the Best Authorities on Vintage motoring in general, and on the *marques* which are illustrated in particular (plus a de-lousing operation by Anthony Bird for which much thanks), the author feels a mild, yet euphoric, sense of irresponsibility. But there are some splendid pictures to make up for it....

A.H.

The Vintage Motor Car, Cecil Clutton and John Stanford, Batsford 1954
The Vintage Motor Car Pocketbook, Cecil Clutton, Paul Bird and Anthony Harding, Batsford 1959
The Sports Car Pocketbook, William Boddy, Batsford 1961
The National Motor Museum Catalogue, 1972 edition
Vintage Cars in Colour, James Barron and D. B. Tubbs, Batsford 1960
Cars of the Connoisseur, J. R. Buckley, Batsford 1960
Classic Car Profiles, Profile Publications 1966–7
The Vintage Car, 1919–1930, T. R. Nicholson, Batsford 1966
Vintage Cars, Cyril Posthumus, Hamlyn 1973
Alfa Romeo, Peter Hull and Roy Slater, Cassell 1964
The Vintage Alvis, Peter Hull and Norman Johnson, Macdonald 1967
The Story of the M.G. Sports Car, F. Wilson McComb, Dent 1972
The Rolls-Royce Motor Car, Anthony Bird and Ian Hallows, Batsford 1964
The Le Mans 24-Hour Race, David Hodges, Temple Press 1963
Land Speed Record, Cyril Posthumus, Osprey 1971

(... and quite a lot of other Best Authorities too!)

Introduction

For some we loved, the loveliest and the best
That from his Vintage rolling Time hath prest.
    Edward Fitzgerald – 'The Rubaiyat of Omar Khayyám'.

Why call them Vintage motor-cars?

The very word 'Vintage' – by virtue of its vinous connotation – implies a product of superior quality. This is confirmed by the Oxford Dictionary's 'wines of well-known vintages', and Chambers' definition of a vintage year being 'one in which a particular product (usually wine) reaches an exceptionally high standard'; or in other words, a product apart from – and a cut above – the common-or-garden, down-to-earth, run-of-the-mill object on sale in any old market place.

The 'Vintage' adjective was not applied to motor-cars before the early or middle 1930s, when a group of young enthusiasts found that the new mass-produced cars they could afford were nasty in most respects, nastier than many of their predecessors in quality, and nastiest of all in performance and handling as they tended to be both slow and flabby. Fortunately for them, there were plenty of good second-hand cars left over from the previous decade, so why, they asked, pay a lot of money for a new and badly-built car when a high-quality one could be had for the proverbial song? These young men, who knew a thing or two about how a car should behave – connoisseurs, to return to the wine analogy – decided to found a club (as Englishmen are wont to do) for the preservation and airing of pre-1931 sports-cars.

The inaugural meeting was held on 23 October 1934, at Harrow in Middlesex, when it was 'decided to hold trials once a month, and Sunday was felt to be a more suitable day than Saturday. It is hoped, particularly, to appeal to owners of 30/98s and 3-litre Bentleys etc.' – a quotation from *Motor Sport* for December 1934, which has a splendid flavour of Surtees' (Robert S. rather than John) Mr Jorrocks and the Surrey Hunt. Initially, when it started life, the Club was known as the Veteran Sports-Car Club, until the Veteran Car Club of Great Britain, which when all is said and done was there first, pointed out that this title could lead to confusion; so it was amicably settled by changing the 'Veteran', very appropriately, to 'Vintage'. The Club started with 73 members – among them such well-known names as Harry Bowler, Cecil 'Sam' Clutton, Tim Carson, Anthony Heal, Forrest Lycett, Laurence Pomeroy Jr and Tom Rolt – who between them owned no fewer than 26 different makes of car. A number of them are still taking part in Vintage motoring events today – and, in 1973, Sam Clutton broke the Edwardian record at Prescott hill-climb in the 1908 Grand Prix Itala with a time of 53.50 seconds in his twenty-fifth year of trying!

How did the cars of which they thought so highly happen to come about?

Some 90 years have gone by since the motor-car first became a practical proposition. Karl Benz was manufacturing cars for sale to the public in 1888, and he continued to make basically the same model for 12 years thereafter. He, and his contemporary designers Daimler, Maybach, de Dion and Bouton, Panhard and Levassor, were all fighting to make their cars work at all at this time. By the mid-1890s they had succeeded, and for the next ten years designers concentrated on making them work fairly reliably, while between about 1906 and 1915 they (particularly Henry Royce, Montague Napier and the Lanchester brothers, Frederick and George) refined them so that they went very well indeed. Nevertheless, good cars were highly expensive and the big, powerful chassis potentially capable of brisk performance were usually bought by rich and elderly people who burdened them with enormously lofty closed bodies, and caused them to be conducted with the sedate dignity they considered proper to their (literally) elevated station. Similar chassis bodied with light, stark, open bodies for the sporting enthusiast were fast and exciting but notably lacking in creature comforts, while the cheaper cars offered little comfort and less performance. In a nutshell, comfortable or exciting motoring, pre-1914, were the perquisites of the well-to-do, and motoring of any sort a convenience of the 'carriage trade'. But the Great War changed all that. . . .

The Armed Services used a wide variety of mechanised transportation of all shapes and sizes: staff cars, tanks, lorries, ambulances – even taxi-cabs when pressed – and thus a vast number of military personnel were brought into close and regular contact with the advantages afforded by the internal combustion engine, and their earlier wonderment was soon dispelled, while many of them actually drove and helped to maintain the machines which they had previously held in awe. When the Armistice was signed in 1918 and demobilisation followed, what could be more natural than that they should aspire to some kind of personal motorised transport of their own?

The motor industry quickly got down to the job of trying to satisfy a car-hungry market. The pre-war manufacturers soon turned over their factories from making munitions and Service vehicles to making cars for sale to the public, and they were hastily joined by many new 'hopefuls' anxious to get into the act and cash in on the demand. The first post-war Motor Show was held at Olympia in 1919 and in *Vintage Cars* (Hamlyn 1973), Cyril Posthumus makes the point that there were more than 40 fresh British names alone, while no less than 272 different manufacturers of all nationalities displayed their wares. It was a roaring success from the salesmen's point of view of the number of orders booked – the prices ranged from £1,850 per chassis (£2,800 with a touring body) for the lordly Rolls-Royce 'Silver Ghost' to £165 for the little belt-driven Tamplin cyclecar, to name examples at either ends of the scale. All the same, it was a long time before some of the customers took delivery of the cars of their choice, for the strikes of the following year, 1920, and particularly those of Midlands foundrymen and pattern makers, caused long delays in the delivery of parts, and pre-war second-hand cars accordingly fetched very high prices. It was a good 18 months before supply caught up with demand and, hardly had this been achieved, than a general trade recession brought about a sharp rise in the cost of living and the spate of orders was reduced to a trickle in 1921/22 with a consequent drop in prices (the little Rover Eight 'light car', for example, went down from £262 to £180). Many of the smaller firms went to the wall, while still more bit the dust in the economic depression of the early thirties, which caused the demise of not far short of half the manufacturers who exhibited at the 1929 Show.

Such is the veneration of Vintage cars today that there is a popular tendency to think that, if a car was made during the Vintage years of 1919 to 1930, then it must be a good one. This is not the case. The Vintage cars' reputations rest squarely on the laurels of the best models in their separate classes, all of which included specimens which are better forgotten – and of which the remark that 'they don't build 'em like that today' should be answered with a firm 'and thank the Lord for that!' For instance most of the cheap cyclecar designs, with the exception of the G.N., ranged from the inefficient and unsound to the downright lethal.

The Vintage car proper was the amalgam of sound design and good materials assembled by skilled labour (which was still relatively cheap), the latter allowing of much hand-finishing and hand-fitting by craftsmen in both the mechanical and body-building departments. It took a comparatively long time to build a Vintage car, and thus the output was small and prices were high by the standards of the mid-seventies. The writer's 1926 14/40 h.p., 2-litre Sunbeam, with a 2-seater drophead body with dickey seat aft, cost £725 when new, which must be comparable to at least £4000 in today's money, i.e. double the price of, say, a Rover 2000, which goes more than twice as fast in greater comfort, and stops immeasurably better . . . but lacks the Sunbeam's 'character'. The Vintage car's appeal today is partly based on the pleasure in owning something which others do not, but a more cogent reason is found in the true Vintage handling characteristics of precise steering, firm road-holding, engine accessibility, and a reasonable amount of performance allied to a 'long-stride', which are endearing qualities not all of which are found in the majority of modern cars, no matter how superior they may be in some other respects.

The downfall of the Vintage car was partly brought about by the world depression of 1929, but much earlier than this Henry Ford with the Model T had been proving that his mass-production, time-and-motion technique produced a lot more cars in the same time for sale at a lower price, and his example was followed by Herbert Austin with his 'Seven' and William Morris and his 'Minor'. Yet the Vintage car itself had been tending to put on a lot of unwanted weight – outside the top echelon – as a result of adopting low-pressure tyres, front-wheel brakes and ever-heavier bodywork necessitating even sturdier chassis.

Grands Cru Classés – the Luxury Cars

In the Edwardian days of motoring, a wealthy owner regarded the driving of his motor-car as a menial job better left to a servant hired specifically for it (together with its maintenance, cleaning and a bit of light gardening on the side). When the war was over and he had been educated a little better in the pleasures and thrills of handling his own thoroughbred machinery, the owner-driver of the top quality car was not content with the stately progression of the ponderous, over-bodied barouches of the earlier days, yet at the same time he saw no reason why he shouldn't motor more briskly in the same sort of comfort. His requirements were soon met by the pre-eminent designers of the Vintage decade, notably Marc Birkigt and W. O. Bentley, both of whom had been responsible for designing aero-engines (and therefore ones at once both light and powerful) during the war years.

In 1919, at the Paris Salon, Birkigt created a sensation when his 37.2 h.p. Hispano-Suiza was exhibited. Its $6\frac{1}{2}$-litre, overhead camshaft, 6-cylinder light-alloy engine was a great advance on anything before it, and produced 135 b.h.p. at only 3,000 r.p.m., which took the car up to 70 to 80 m.p.h. depending on bodywork. Road-holding and steering were excellent for a large car and the appearance was superb. Its splendid 4-wheel-brakes were powered by a unique mechanical servo mechanism good enough to be adopted, under licence, by Rolls-Royce when they at last fitted 4-wheel-brakes to the old 'Silver Ghost' in 1924. This great car, which was built in both France and Spain, was years ahead of its time and set the target for others to try to match during the whole of the Vintage years.

Rolls-Royce entered the period with their well-appreciated 40/50 h.p. 'Silver Ghost', with but detail changes, and it continued to sell well (still at £1850 for a chassis only) until it was replaced by the first of a new line – the Phantom I – in 1925. This was an excellent motor-car with an engine of 7668 c.c. producing about 100 b.h.p. and capable of around 80 m.p.h. with touring coachwork. In 1929 this model was itself superseded by the Phantom II – another of the great Vintage cars.

The giant of the twenties was the Bugatti Type 41 or 'Royale'. This vast and beautifully-engineered car had a straight-eight engine of no less than 12,760 c.c., which produced around 300 b.h.p. at 2,000 r.p.m., and the engine itself was 4 ft 7 in long. The wheelbase was 14 ft 2 in and the track 5 ft 3 in, yet in spite of its bulk, the 'Royale' weighed in at a mere 45 cwt. Maximum speed was in the 110 to 120 m.p.h. bracket. It was built for sale to Royalty and Heads of State alone, and only six were made.

The leading American upholders of prestige motoring were the Duesenberg brothers, Frederick and August, who made a superlatively designed and very well-built luxury car bearing their own name. This was again a straight-eight – the favourite lay-out for cars of high-performance during the Vintage years in both the racing and top-price fields – of just on 7-litres capacity and said to produce some 265 b.h.p. at 4,200 r.p.m. (there is some scepticism about this however) with twin overhead-camshafts and hydraulic brakes. This was the famous Model J (which had been preceded by the less-exciting Model A of 4.26-litres producing 92 b.h.p.). Unfortunately few Duesenbergs crossed the Atlantic as, with duties paid, they not only cost more than their European rivals, but were neither as refined nor as well finished.

Italy's entrant for the Grand Luxe Stakes was the Tipo 8A Isotta Fraschini, another straight-eight of 6-litres. It rivalled the *panache* of Hispano-Suiza in name alone, as it couldn't hold a camshaft to it from a performance point of view. It had pushrod-operated overhead valves and the depressing output for its capacity of 80 b.h.p. allied to a weight of getting on for three tons. However, by 1925 it contrived to produce 120 b.h.p. from its now bored-out engine of 7372 c.c. Masses of low-speed torque and a flat power-curve were the chief qualities of the Isotta which make it a fine 'single-gear' motor-car; this was as well because it was marred by a three-speed gearbox with ill-chosen ratios. It could be started from rest in top gear, whence it would proceed to some 80 m.p.h. with reasonable alacrity in a refined manner. This suited some people but not the connoisseurs, who bought Hispanos instead. Nevertheless, the Isotta was a very impressive-looking car when bodied by the best Italian and French coachbuilders, and it sold reasonably well in these countries – and particularly to Hollywood, U.S.A. . . .

These marques were the outstanding *haute vie* cars from five countries and two continents in the twenties. Space permits no more than a mention of a few of their rivals, but a step down the ladder, which were very fine luxury machines in their own rights: the Lanchester 40 (G.B.), Napier 40/50 (G.B.), Daimler Double-six (G.B.), Lincoln V-8 (U.S.A.); Packard side-valve straight-eight (U.S.A.), 24-valve, six-cylinder Pierce-Arrow (U.S.A.) and the sleeve-valve V-12 Voisin (France).

Cru Bourgeois – the Economy Cars

Leaving the Sublime for a 'bit-of-the-other', the delightfully uncluttered, if indifferently surfaced, roads of the Vintage period were mainly populated by the worthy, if rather dull, Morris Bull-noses, Clynos, light Humbers, Trojans, Austin Heavy Twelve Fours and Sevens, Model T Fords and their like, whilst the 30/98 Vauxhalls, the Bentleys, the Lagondas and such exotica, dashed past one comparatively rarely. Cecil Clutton and John Stanford point out in *The Vintage Motor Car* (Batsford 1954), while Morris made 750 cars a week in 1924, only 500 30/98s and under 100 Aston Martins were made in the Vintage years.

These were the sensible, if pedestrian, utility cars which made up the transportation of the bread-and-butter motoring public of the 1920s, which was of course but a small fraction of that of the sixties and seventies. That they were soundly built is proved by the number which enjoy cherished survival today in the hands of members of the V.S.C.C.

(though the most doting owner would hardly contend that they are 'sports-cars'), while the ephemeral construction of the *Cru Artisan,* or blown-together, exiguous cyclecars, is equally underlined by their almost non-existent representation save for a handful of G.N.s and a few single examples of Tamplin, A. V. Monocar and the like.

Premier Cru – the Middle-price Tourers and Saloons

These cars are typical of the upper-middle-class products of the Vintage years, though the v.s.c.c. took little interest in them during the thirties, when far more exciting cars were available at no great cost. Nevertheless, the post-1939/45-war explosion of interest in the soundly-engineered cars of earlier days has ensured the preservation of a wide cross-section of the better makes of the twenties – which have survived the lack of interest, or even neglect, of their 1930s owners by virtue of their original dreadnought architecture.

The Sunbeams, which were manufactured in works at Wolverhampton are outstanding and have always been in a (rather higher) class of their own, thus providing the pinnacle of Vintage touring cars and ensuring them a following since the Company's demise in 1935. In their time you might just mention them in the same breath as the 20 h.p. Rolls-Royce without fear of *lèse-majesté*. We do not, of course, include the later Rootes-product of the same name but dissimilar qualities. Slightly less distinguished parcels to be put down in this bin would include the Alvis 12/50, the 6-cylinder A.C.s, the smaller Vauxhalls (14/40s), the Meadows-engined Lea-Francis, 6-cylinder 20/55 Humbers and the excellent Riley 'Nines'.

The Continental *marques* in this class – Delage, Ballot, Lancia, Panhard, O.M., Mors, Voisin, Chenard-et-Walcker – tended to outperform the home product, as English traffic was notoriously slow, whilst in France and Italy there was (a) less of it, and (b) the roads encouraged a leaden-footed approach to driving and a higher top-gear ratio.

Vive le Sport!

Sports-cars originally made up the foundations of the v.s.c.c., though times have changed somewhat and its members today cast their nets much wider.

In the twenties the enthusiastic sporting motorist had a very wide range of cars from which to choose, both from the cubic capacity and price points of view. Amongst the British manufacturers, the kings of the Vintage sports-cars were the 30/98 Vauxhall Velox and the various, legendary, Bentleys of 3, 4½, 6½ and 8-litres, of which the 4½ was probably the best 'all-rounder'. The Vauxhall was a 'production' version of a pre-war car specially designed for hill-climbing events by L. H. Pomeroy, while the Bentleys were entirely new designs from the board of Walter Owen Bentley, who had been responsible for two successful rotary aero-engines during the war. The stirring saga of the Bentleys' victories at Le Mans are part of our motoring heritage. A notch lower in the hierarchy came the 3-litre Sunbeam, the Aston Martin, the S-type Invicta, 2-litre Lagonda and the chain-driven Frazer Nash with its 12 h.p. Anzani engine. But these were all expensive cars to buy, and the less well-heeled enthusiasts got a great deal of fun from the 14/40 and M-type M.G.s (both closely based on models in the ordinary Morris domestic range) and the sporting versions of the Austin Seven.

Continental contenders were headed by the Teutonic, thunderous, seven-litres of the supercharged Mercedes-Benz of vast proportions and superb presence. Italy went in for rather more finesse as exemplified by the exquisitely-made 1500 and 1750 c.c. Alfa Romeos designed by Vittorio Jano, and the very forward-looking Lancia Lambda which had i.f.s. and an integral chassis in 1922. The *tricolore* was upheld by Bugatti with his fine series of sporting cars (Types 40, 44 and 49), with some worthy backing-up from Delage and Voisin. France also produced a number of excellent small-capacity sports-cars (of about 1100 c.c.) of which Amilcar and Salmson sold briskly, with a fair number crossing the Channel.

Grands Prix

After the Armistice, Grand Prix road-racing did not get started until 1921, when the French G.P. was held over a course at Le Mans. An American 3-litre Duesenberg shook everyone by beating the fancied French Ballots, who nevertheless won the Italian Grand Prix later in the year. For 1922 it was the Fiat team, with their 6-cylinder cars, which was the most successful, as they were again the following season with supercharged straight-eights, though H. O. D. Segrave's Sunbeam took the French G.P. at Tours when the Fiats' superchargers gave trouble. Segrave did it again next year on a Sunbeam in the Spanish G.P. but without the opposition of the P.2 Alfa Romeos which proved unbeatable elsewhere during the 1924 season.

The V-12 Delages were given superchargers for 1925 (an example competes in Vintage racing today) and were a near-match for the P.2 Alfa Romeos but, though close racing seemed ensured, true confrontation was not forthcoming, while Fiat did not race and Sunbeam were outclassed. The 1926 and 1927 Grands Prix were contested mainly by French cars – Type 35 Bugattis, Delages and Talbot-Darracqs – under a new 1½-litre Formula for which all three *marques* came out with blown straight-eights, with the honours going to Bugatti in 1926 and Delage in 1927.

For the premier form of motoring competition, racing was at a low ebb between 1927 and 1930, and the Grands Prix were run as *Formule Libre*. No new cars materialised, the 1½-litre Delages did not appear – though the V-12s did and the P.2 Alfas beat them – and the whole affair degenerated into something of a Bugatti benefit. The final year of the decade heralded the arrival on the scene of a new car from Maserati of Bologna, with a blown 2½-litre straight-eight engine, which won five times and dominated the season – and made the others decide that they had better go away and think again! The end of the Vintage decade thus marked the moment for a new departure in racing car design.

The major moments and events of the Vintage period of 1919 to 1930 have now been lightly sketched in, but record-breaking has not been mentioned. Suffice to say that the World Land Speed Record in 1919 stood to Ralph de Palma's Packard at 149.875 m.p.h., and in 1929 to Henry Segrave's 'Golden Arrow' at 231.446 m.p.h. In between, the Roll includes Tommy Milton (Duesenberg), K. Lee Guinness (Sunbeam), René Thomas (Delage), Ernest Eldridge (Fiat), Malcolm Campbell (Sunbeam and 'Bluebird'), J. G. Parry Thomas (Higham Special 'Babs') and Ray Keech (Triplex), all names which stir the blood of the middle-aged today! Motor racing thrived in the Vintage years at Brooklands, which re-opened in 1920.

The Vintage Car Movement flourishes now as never before. The Vintage Sports-Car Club has some 6,000 members owning about 160 makes of car against its 73 founder members in 1934. Vintage cars are bought and sold for as many thousands of pounds as they were considered worth hundreds in the early 1960s – and tenners before the Second World War. Well might one reflect upon the well-known dictum of Sir Frederick Henry Royce: 'the quality will remain when the price is forgotten'.

The wheel is well past full-circle perhaps?

1920 ROLLS-ROYCE 'SILVER GHOST'

It was upon the solid foundation of the conventional, but superbly-made, chassis of the 40/50 h.p. 'Silver Ghost' that the fortunes of the greatest of all *marques* rested and flourished for 16 years, starting in 1906 when their 'one-model' policy began.

The 7.4-litre, L-head side-valve engine had its six cast-iron cylinders in two groups of three. In accordance with their clients' requirements of a luxury carriage in the Edwardian and Vintage periods, Rolls-Royce's trump card was fantastic flexibility, in silence and without vibration. Thus the 'Silver Ghost' would pull happily from 3 m.p.h. to 70 in top gear, while returning a consumption of 16 to 20 m.p.g. The car spent most of its production life without front-wheel brakes, but these eventually came in 1924 (see page 9).

The legendary reputation of the 'Silver Ghost' stems from an output of but 7,876 specimens – 1,703 being made between 1921 and 1926 at the Rolls-Royce factory at Springfield, Massachusetts, U.S.A., and the remainder at the English works at Derby. Nevertheless it was probably the greatest of the Edwardian designs, and one which was able to hold its own until the mid-Vintage years when it was phased out in favour of the first of the 'Phantom' line, which was launched in 1925 (see page 36).

Photo: National Motor Museum

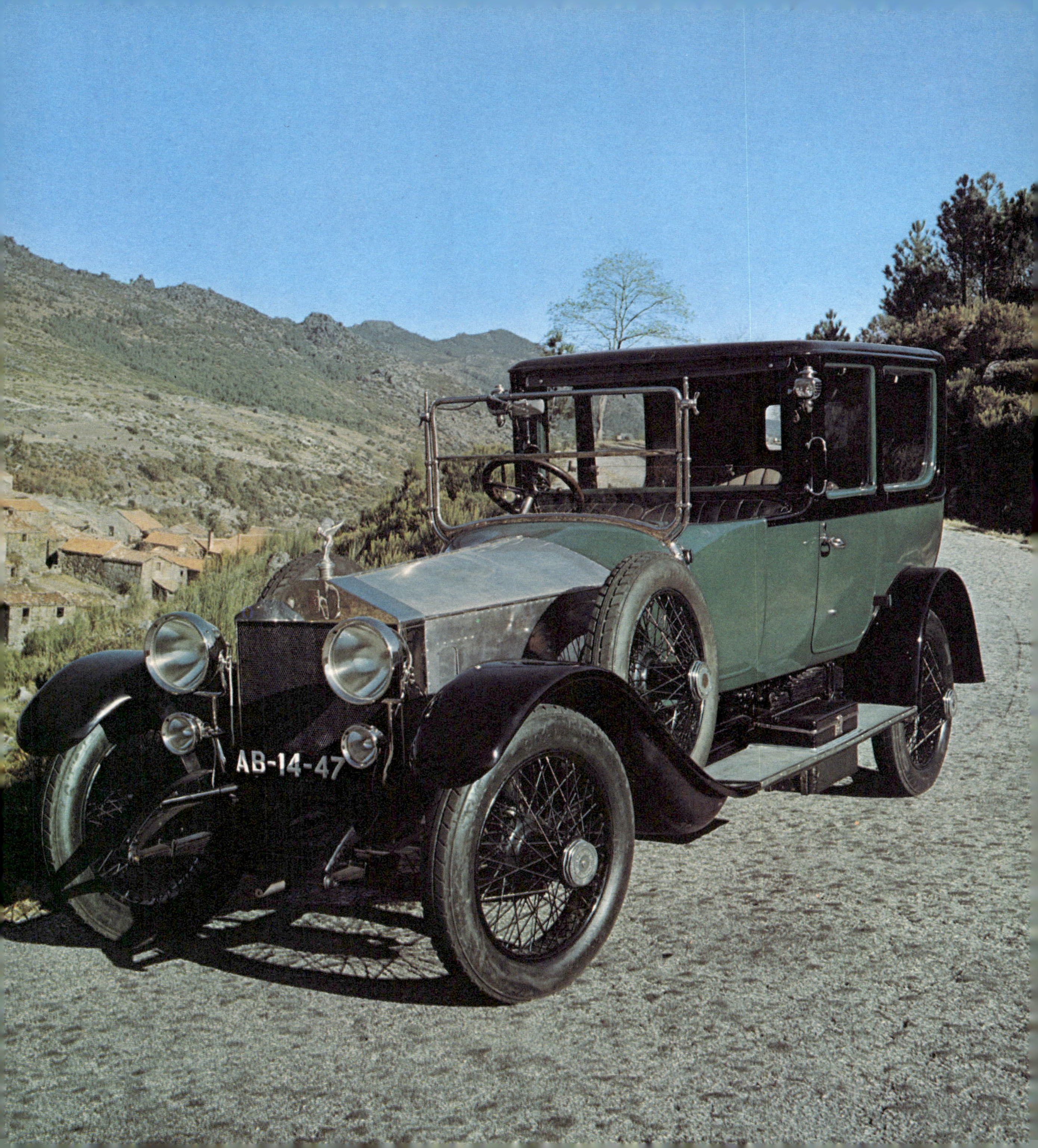
AB-14-47

1920 ROVER EIGHT

The Rover Company's first motor-car – a single cylinder effort – was produced in 1905, but by the outbreak of the Great War in 1914 they had made a name for themselves with sound, solid, four-cylinder tourers; and they also, somewhat surprisingly, won the Tourist Trophy of 1907.

When the war was over, they decided to have a tilt at the light car market, and brought out their 8 h.p. 'economy' model. This had a horizontally-opposed, twin-cylinder air-cooled engine of about a litre, a three-speed box and worm drive. Its chassis was crude even for a cheap car of the time, but the cheeky-looking little car with the disc wheels sold briskly, with its very reasonable performance of about 50 m.p.g. and 45 m.p.h. top speed, which was allied to passable acceleration and hill-climbing qualities. It was murmured that some early specimens had a tendency to lose their cylinder-heads (glowing a cheerful, Christmassy bright red the while!) at high revs., but one suspects that the story must have gained somewhat in the telling. . . .

Anyway, the Eight survived until 1925, when it was replaced by a water-cooled four-cylinder model of similar engine capacity and staid demeanour. People who wanted basic motoring obviously preferred the Austin Seven (see page 26) which was quieter, more conventional-looking and marked a break-away from the cyclecar image of the Rover with its big air-cooled 'flat twin' engine.

Photo: Autocar

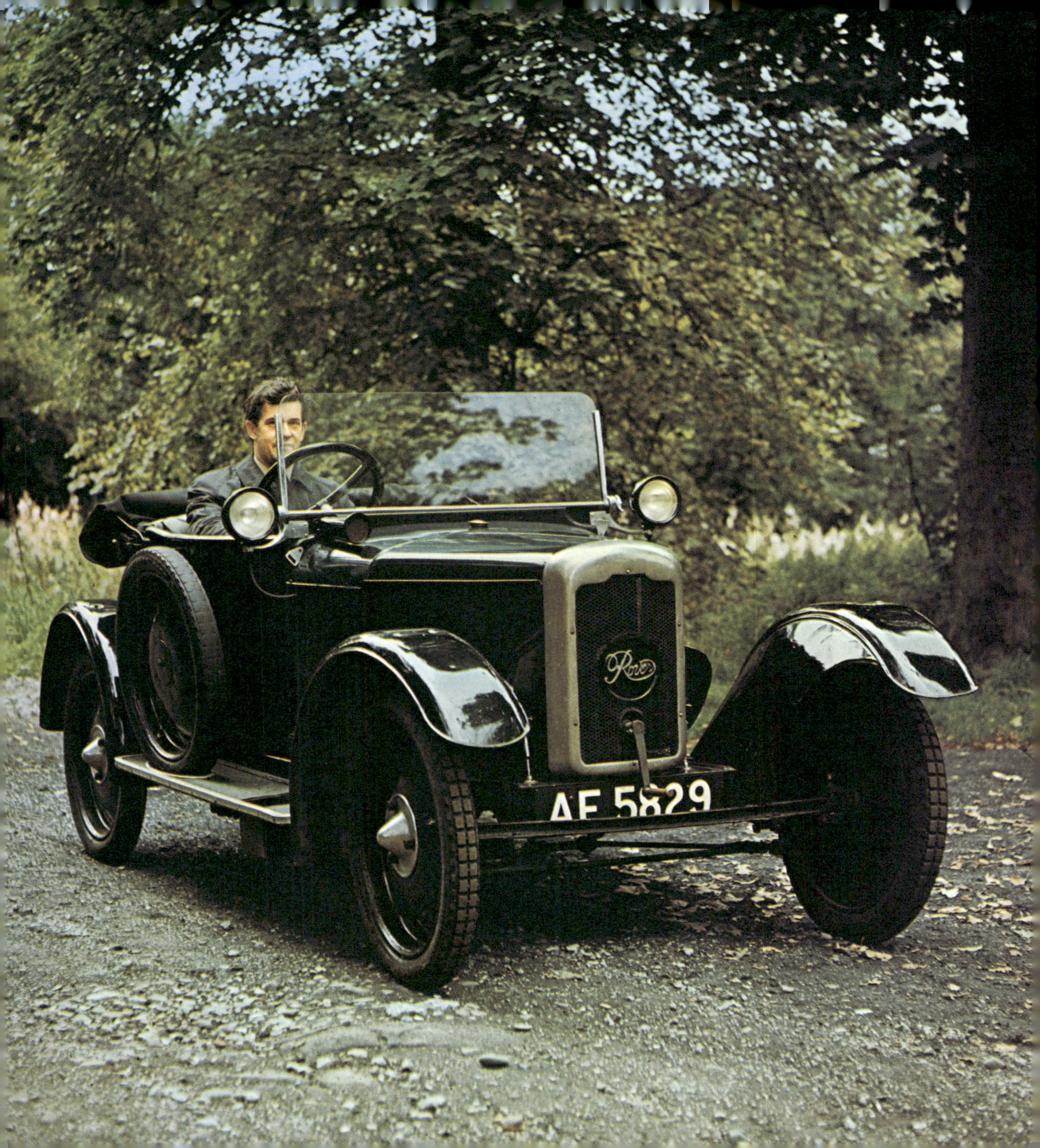
Rover
AE 5829

1920 STANLEY 735-A

The identical twins, F. E. and F. O. Stanley of Newton, Massachusetts, founded their steam car company in 1897. By 1899 they had sold out for a good figure and the cars came to be known as Locomobiles, though the Stanleys were still there as general managers. By 1903, however, the astute brothers were back at the top of the pack and manufacturing a twin-cylinder car with the engine geared straight on to the back axle, under their own name; in 1906 the brave, redoubtable Fred Marriott took the World's Land Speed Record in a special version at 127 m.p.h. – and nearly killed himself in the following year trying to better it.

These were the exciting, stimulating days of the Stanley steamers – those before the fast-driving brothers retired, in 1918, and their company was taken over by an industrial group.

The car illustrated was once owned by Sir Richard Fairey, of aircraft manufacturing fame. Under the bonnet is a vertical fire-tube boiler (which takes quite a while to brew-up) and its condenser looks like a conventional radiator. The fuel was kerosene which was then cheaper than petrol; and this was just as well because, like all steam cars, the Stanley had a he-man's thirst.

The Vintage Stanleys were sound, staid-looking vehicles of good performance with delightful smoothness, but requiring considerable patience in the mornings! However, enough placid people appreciated their manner-of-going to keep the company alive until 1926.

Photo: National Motor Museum

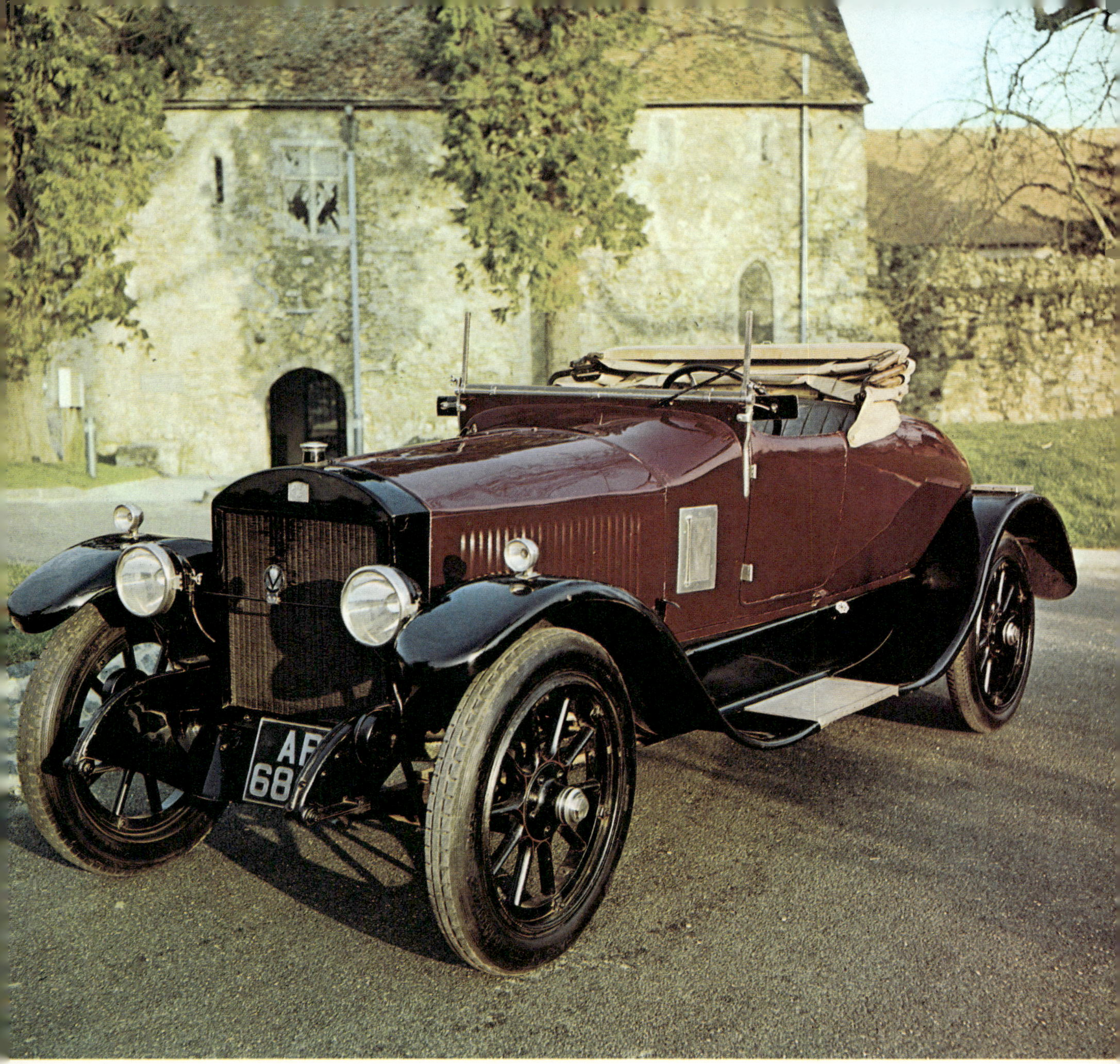

1921 CITROËN TYPE A 10CV

André Citroën was to France as Herbert Austin and Henry Ford were to Britain and the U.S.A., in that it was he who brought cheap motoring to the peasants of France.

During the war he was a very large and successful manufacturer of munitions, but at one time, earlier on, he was chief engineer of the Mors Company. Citroën made a study of American mass-production techniques, which he then proceeded to employ after the Armistice, in the production of his first model, the Type A, which came out in 1919. The little 4-cylinder 1.3-litre car had a three-speed gearbox and rear-wheel brakes only. It was soundly built – as it needed to be in the agricultural districts of France – and its sales were backed-up by Citroën depots all over the country which charged a fixed sum for servicing. At its price of around 8,000 francs it only cost about as much as was being demanded for some of its ephemeral cyclecar contemporaries, but it must be admitted that the performance was not exactly exhilarating, as the Citroën 10CV was hard pressed to make 40 m.p.h. without a decent downhill slope to assist it. All the same, it provided economical transport for many thousands of Frenchmen who would otherwise have had to stick to hay-burning motive power on their journeyings.

The beautifully restored car opposite is on show at the Egeskov Museum in Denmark.

Photo: National Motor Museum

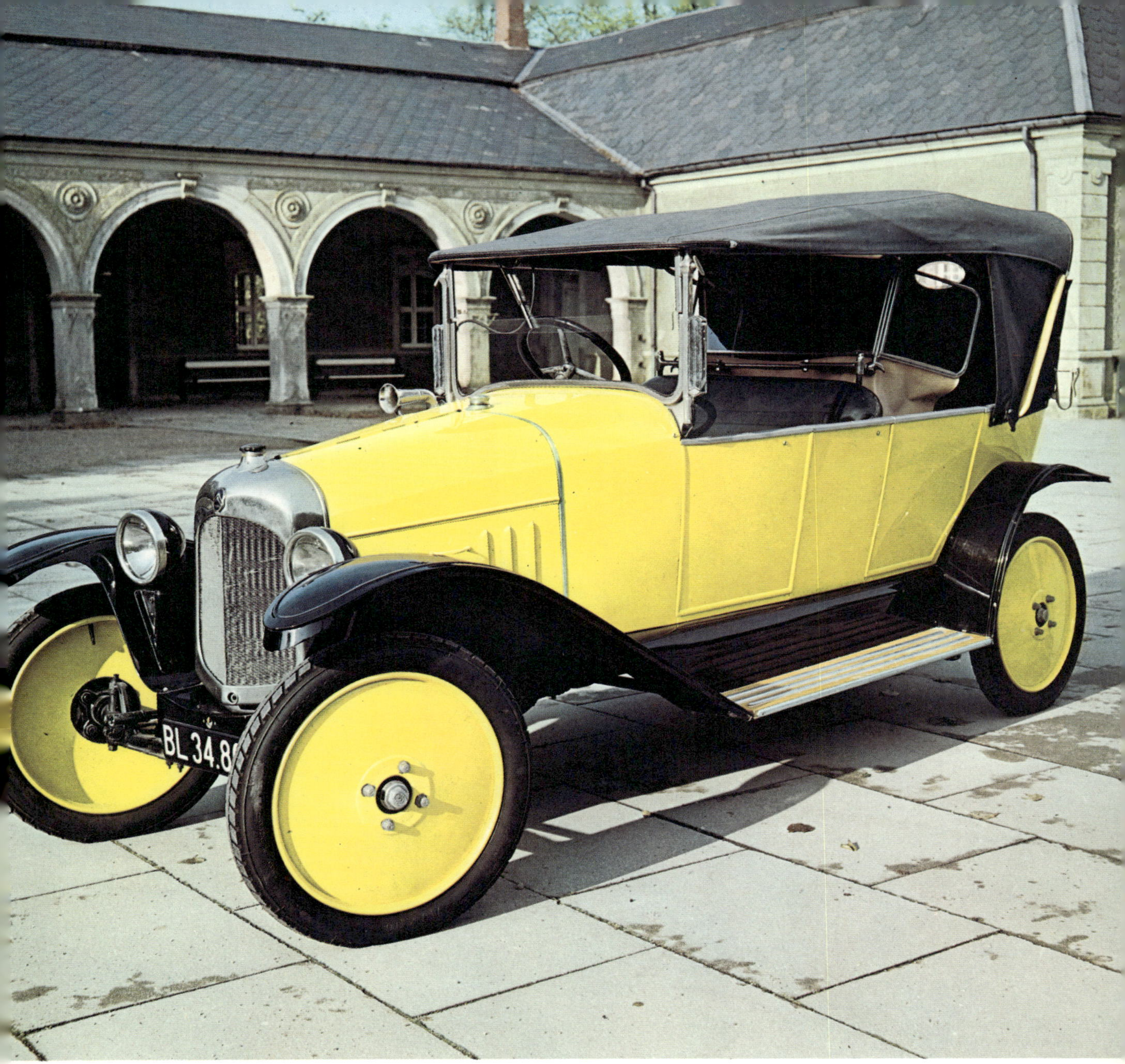
BL 34.8

1921 A.C. 11.9 h.p.

This pleasant little high-quality Vintage light tourer is from the Montagu Collection in the National Motor Museum.

The initials A.C. stand for Auto Carrier – a company which started in 1908 and built a three-wheeler commercial van, which was followed by a two-seater passenger version called the 'Sociable'. These were made up to the 1914–18 war. They also got out a four-wheeler in 1913, but this was not in serious production until 1918, when it was an immediate success at around £560, thanks to its fine appearance and performance and excellent finish. It had a four-cylinder, side-valve Anzani engine of $1\frac{1}{2}$-litres capacity, a three-speed gearbox on the back axle and a transmission disc brake, though the latter was not really up to its job, causing one of the works competition drivers to state that it was only fit for making toast. . . .

The four-cylinder car was kept in production until 1927–28 when it was dropped, the firm concentrating on its excellent six-cylinder model which was to have the remarkable production run of over 40 years, from 1919 to 1963. The company still makes expensive sports-cars at one end of the scale and three-wheeled invalid cars at the other, in its works at Thames Ditton in Surrey.

Photo: National Motor Museum

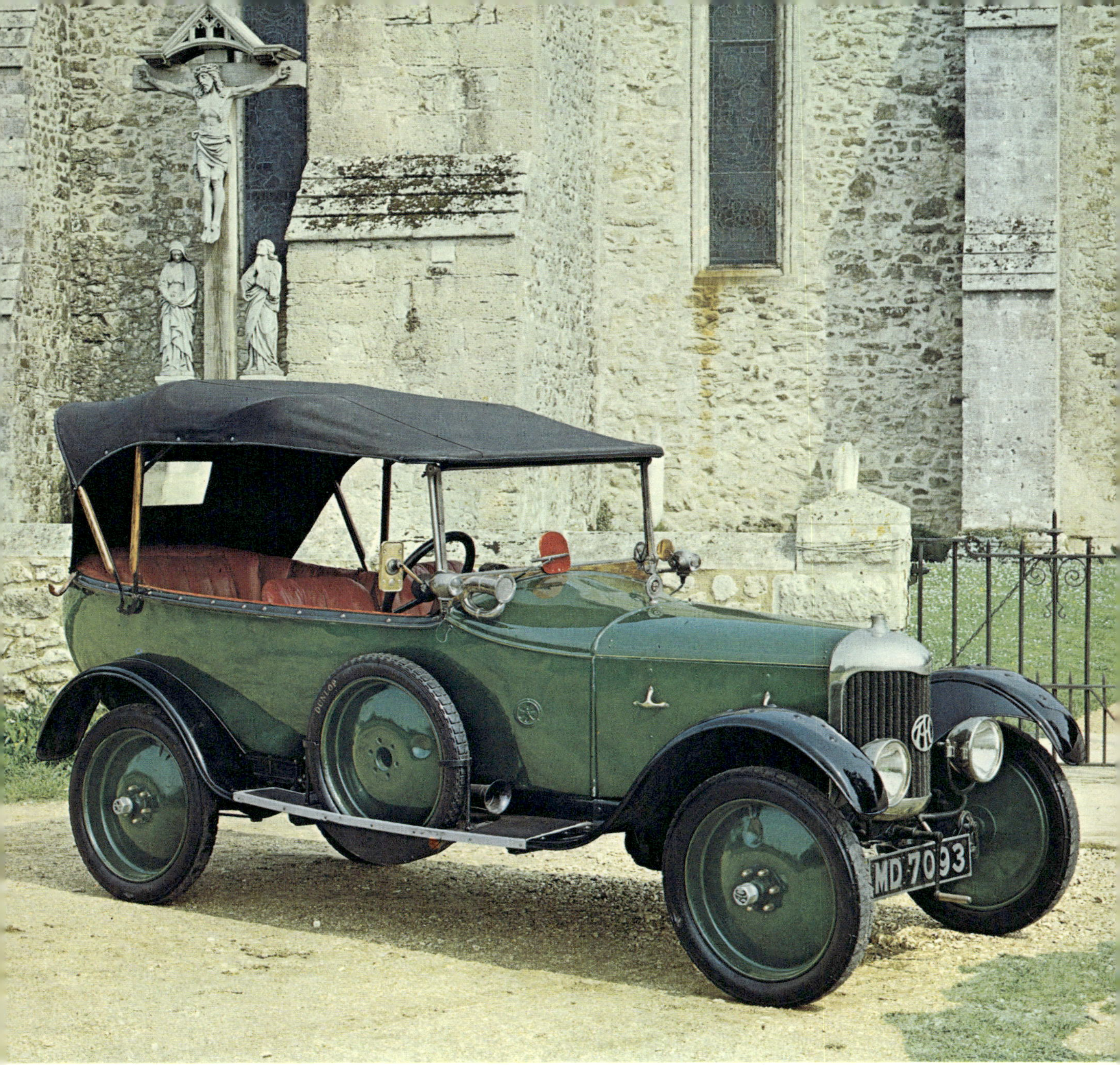
MD 7093

1923 AUSTIN SEVEN

The Austin Motor Company's catalogue introduces their praiseworthy small car more successfully than yards of new prose: '... introduced to supersede the sidecar combination ... an ideal car for a woman to use herself ... everyone is brought within the hood (viz. no dickey seats) ... enables the executive to make the utmost use of his time, while his expenditure is no more than tram or bus fares ... a car for the commercial traveller, who can penetrate into districts which poor train services would hardly make it worth his while to cover.' The message is complete!

The Austin Seven was introduced in 1922, and it ousted the crude, impractical cyclecars of the early 1920s. In effect it was the first car to be specifically designed as a small, scaled-down, reasonably comfortable version of its heavier and more expensive Big Brethren. Its 4-cylinder side-valve engine (56 × 76 mm) of 747 ccs. produced 10.5 h.p. at 2,500 r.p.m. With its 8½ cwt, this gave the cobby little beast a top speed of 50 m.p.h., a consumption of 45/60 m.p.g. according to how it was driven – and so well was it made that it was practically indestructible. From 1924 the Sevens had electric starting and lighting, and from 1923, brakes of a kind on all four wheels. Strictly speaking this was not, at first, a four-wheel brake system as the foot brake took effect only on the hind wheels whilst the hand brake discouraged the front ones. However, determined application of both brakes simultaneously in Surrey would, as a disgruntled critic observed, prevent the car plunging into the sea off the Sussex coast. In 1923 the price was £165 but by 1929 this had got down to £125. No wonder they sold. ...

In its various forms of development the Seven survived in production until 1938, by which time over a quarter-of-a-million of them had been built. Clutton and Stanford go so far as to say that the Austin Seven is 'one of the immortal designs in motoring history'.

Photo: National Motor Museum

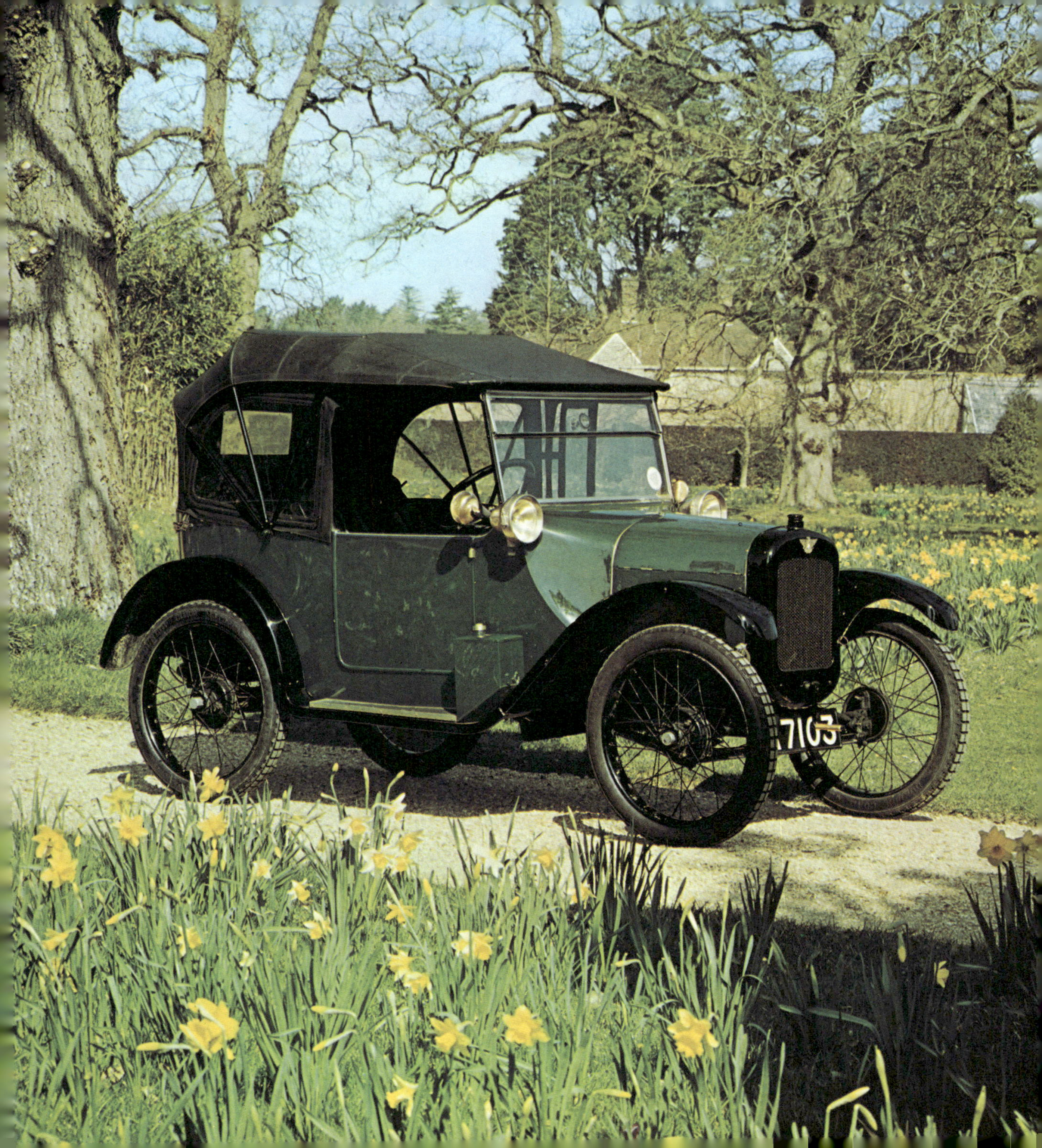
7103

1923 37.2 h.p. HISPANO-SUIZA H6B

The Hispano-Suizas were made in both France and Spain, and their designer was the great Swiss engineer, Marc Birkigt. Although his cars achieved considerable success before the 1914–18 war, it was the 37.2 h.p. which brought the *marque* true international acclaim when it was first shown at the Paris Salon of November 1919.

This model was known in France as the '32-CVH6' and in Spain as the Type 41. In its design, Birkigt was able to draw upon his wide experience of aero-engine design and construction – his engines were used in S.E.5 and S.P.A.D. fighters during the war. The latter aircraft were flown by the French ace Capitaine Georges Guynemer and his pilots, who carried a flying stork emblem as their squadron insignia which was used after the war on the Hispano-Suiza as its radiator mascot. The car's outstanding features were the $6\frac{1}{2}$-litre, overhead camshaft, light-alloy engine with two plugs per cylinder, and the gearbox-driven servo operating the four-wheel brakes (see page 9). There was a three-speed gearbox in unit with the engine and dual coil ignition with automatic advance and retard. Although versions with larger engines were to be produced in later years, the '32-CVH6' was available from the French factory until 1934.

The very handsome example illustrated carries a dual-cowl, four-seater, phaeton tourer body with boat-tail, by Michel Gillet of Paris.

Photo: Roger McDonald

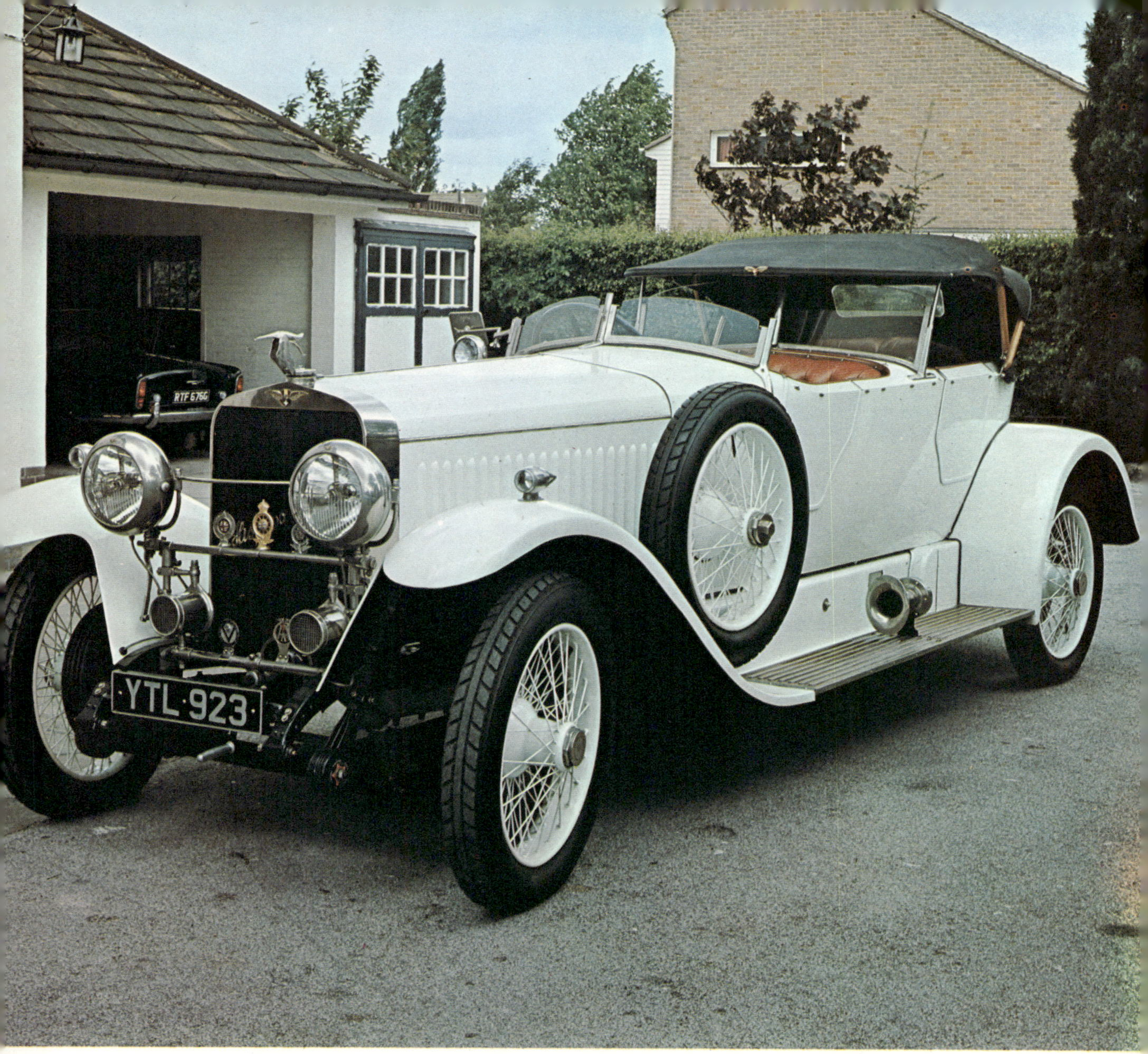
YTL 923
RTF 676G

1924 MORRIS 'COWLEY'

Many Cowmen would be surprised to learn that the famous 'Bull-nose' Morris in its original form – as manufactured in 1915 when it first appeared – was really as much an American car as an English one (engine, gearbox, axles), and thereafter that it was an efficient hotch-potch of bought-out components. All the same, it was with this car that William Morris did his share of bringing 'Motoring for the Masses' of Britain in the early and middle twenties.

The 'Cowley' was preceded by his very similar design, the 'Oxford' model of 1913, but the war stopped supplies of its White and Poppe (of Coventry) engine, so Morris turned to importing 'Continental' engines, modified to suit his requirements, from Detroit, as the U.S.A. were not as yet at war. After the Armistice, he arranged for much the same engine to be manufactured in a Coventry factory set up during the war to make Hotchkiss guns; hence the popular misconception that the bullet-nosed Morris had a Hotchkiss engine. It was a 4-cylinder unit of 1550 ccs. producing 25 b.h.p., which enabled the 'Cowley' – which was a cheaper (by £60) version of the 'Oxford' – to bowl happily along at about 50 m.p.h. and for about 30 miles to each inexpensive gallon of the day.

It sold well from the beginning, and very well indeed when Morris reduced his prices at a time when other manufacturers were raising theirs. A 'Cowley' cost £465 in 1921, £225 in 1923, and a mere £175 in 1925 – and it was always first-class in quality of manufacture and also in manner-of-going.

No wonder, therefore, that 54,151 drivers bought 'Cowleys' in 1925, and many more thousands thereafter, thus ensuring that the 'Bull-noses' are remembered with affectionate nostalgia by so many elderly motorists today.

Photo: National Motor Museum

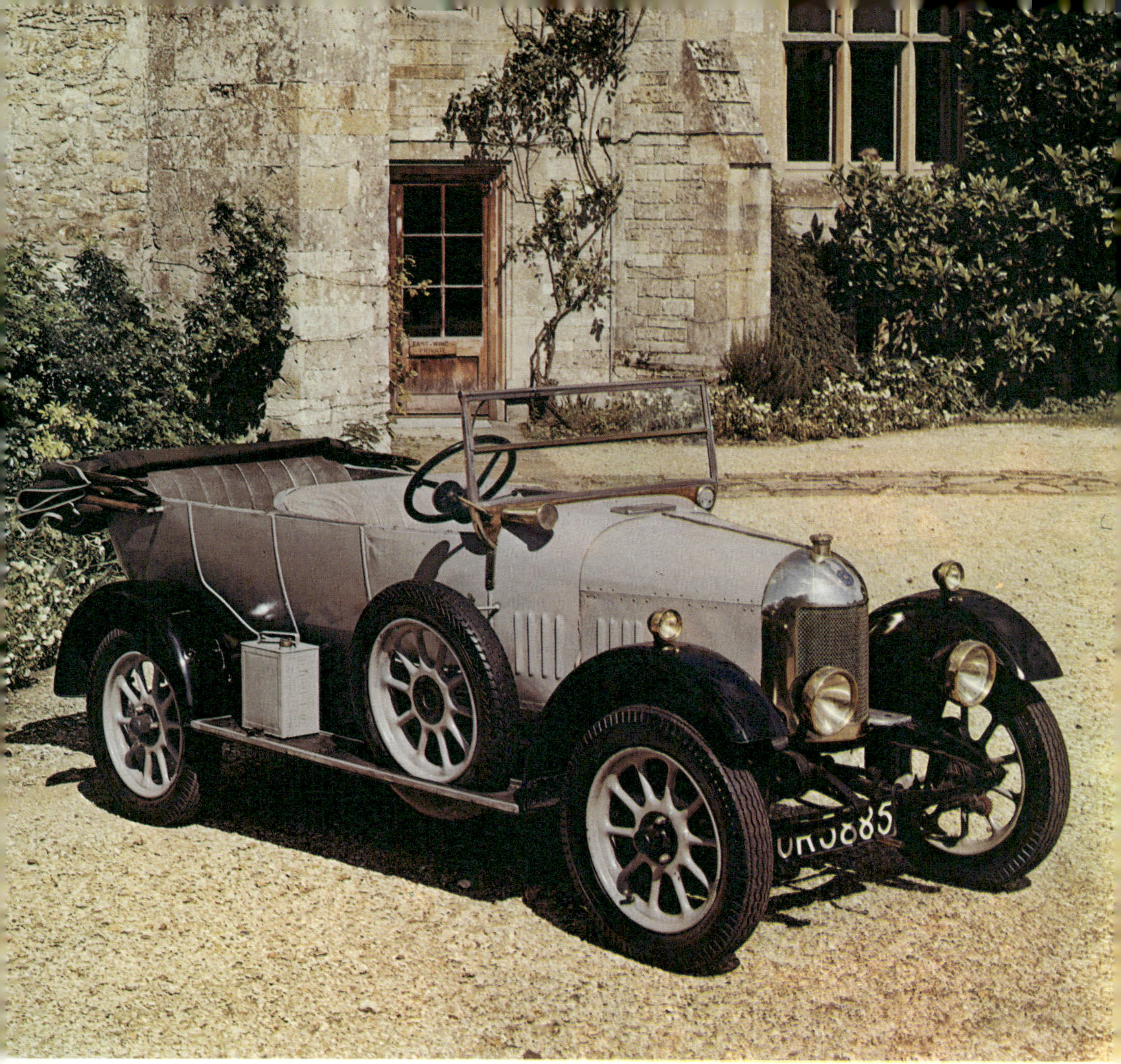

1924 VAUXHALL 30/98

In 1913 J. Higginson of Stockport (who, incidentally, invented the 'Autovac') asked Vauxhall Motors and Laurence Pomeroy Senior, to build him a special car of high performance with which to take the Shelsley Walsh hill-climb record. They produced a car with a four-cylinder side-valve engine of 4½ litres (98 × 150 mm), giving about 90 b.h.p. at 2,800 r.p.m., which was based on the earlier, successful, 1910 3-litre 'Prince Henry' model. This was fitted into a light chassis similar to that of the Coupe de l'Auto racing cars, with engine and gearbox mounted in a sub-frame, and rear-wheel brakes only. Pomeroy and Vauxhall did their work well and the car obliged at Shelsley.

After the war, in 1919, it was put into production and was known as the 30/98, or E-type, Vauxhall. Its manufacturers claimed that it was 'a sporting car which has never known a superior', and it certainly performed very pleasantly with a top speed in the middle 80s carrying a four-seater touring body.

Late in 1922 the revised 'OE' model appeared. The engine was now converted to pushrod-operated overhead valves, and the stroke had been shortened to 140 mm. In this new form it produced some 110 b.h.p. at 3,500 r.p.m. In 1923 some rather unsatisfactory front-wheel brakes were added. These were changed to an erratic hydraulic system in 1927, when a balanced crankshaft improved the output to 120 b.h.p. Production stopped in the same year when Vauxhall Motors were taken over by the American General Motors Corporation.

The 30/98 was one of the great sporting cars of the Vintage decade, combining a first-class performance for the time with great flexibility and charm. Some 580 cars were built in all.

Photo: London Art Tech

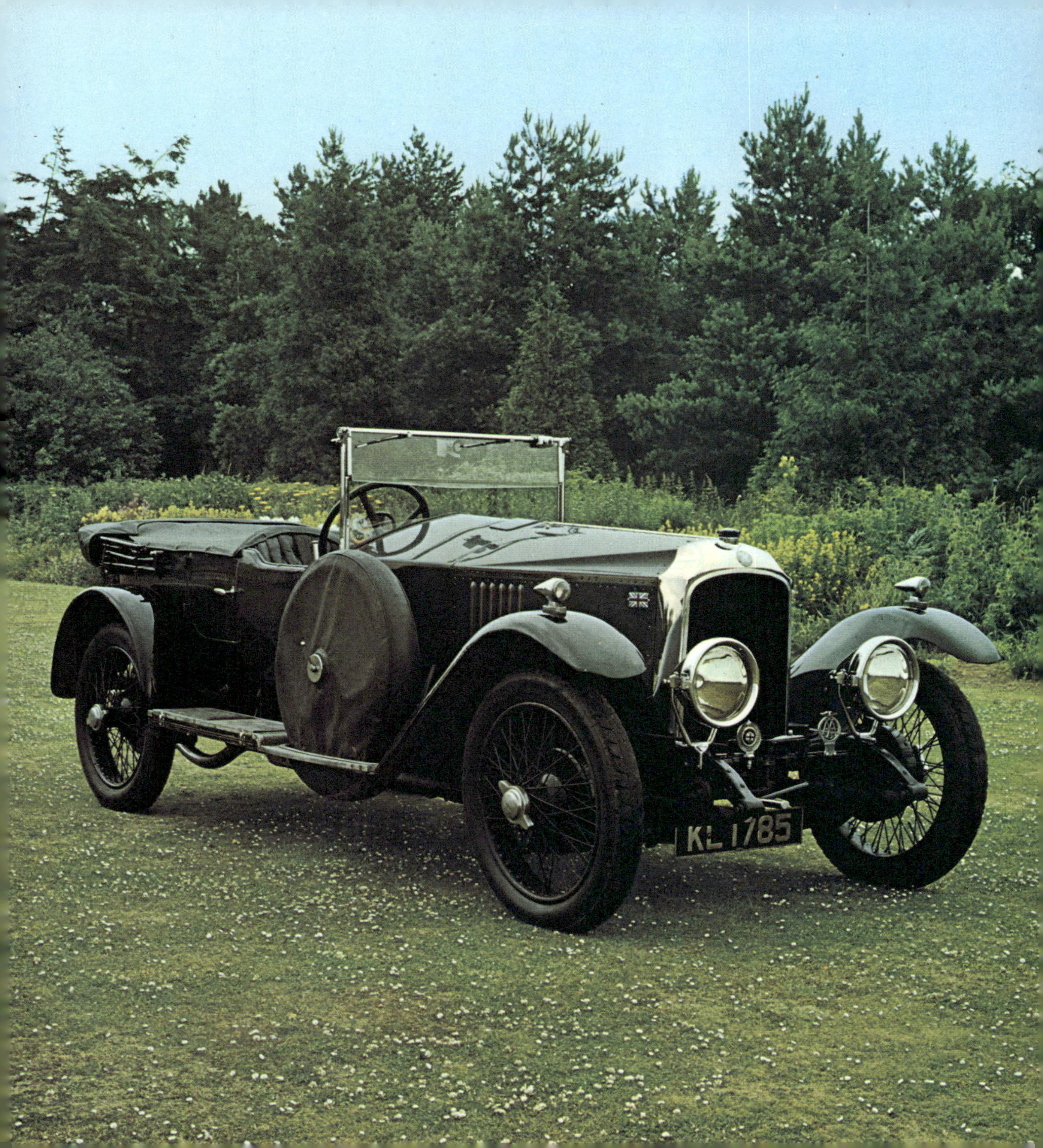
KL 1785

1925 FORD MODEL T

Over a period of 19 years – from 1908 to 1927 – Henry Ford contrived to sell 15,007,033 examples of a rather bad design of car, light van or truck, which he had built in factories in the U.S.A., Canada and Manchester, England.

The Model T, or 'Tin Lizzie' as she was affectionately dubbed, burst upon the motoring scene in October 1908. In touring guise she cost $850 (£170) in 1909, but by 1916 a similarly-bodied car was down to $360, thanks to a one-model policy and Ford's new 'Mass Production' techniques.

The car, which was designed by Joseph Galamb and C. H. Wills under Ford's direction, had a 4-cylinder engine of 2.9 litres, pedal-operated 'high', 'low' and reverse speeds by epicyclic gears, transverse suspension and rear wheel brakes, while the steering was somewhat uncertain if 'Lizzie' was pressed near to her maximum velocity of 45 to 50 m.p.h.

'Lizzie' was no beauty, but for all her crudity of design and uncouth aspect, she was a well-built girl and a faithful friend, which endeared her to millions of owners. After 1913, Henry Ford said that you could have her in any colour you liked provided it was black. . . .

The Model T Ford had more impact on the world's population – and particularly on that of the U.S.A. – than any other car of any age. It was one of the all-time greats.

Photo: National Motor Museum

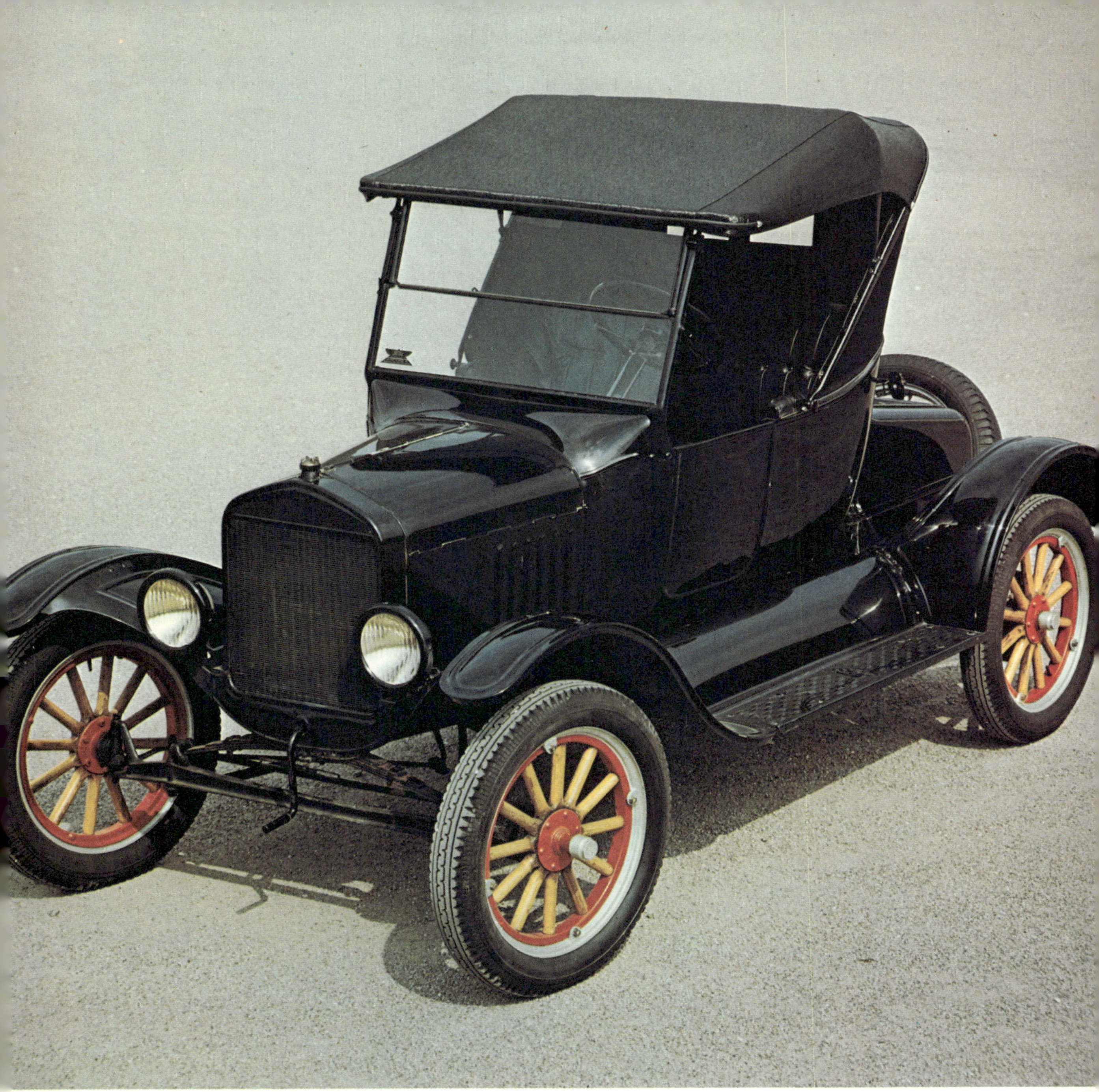

1925 ROLLS-ROYCE 'PHANTOM I'

After the war, Rolls-Royce continued to produce their Edwardian masterpiece, the 'Silver Ghost', which had first been introduced in 1906 (see page 16). It was therefore hardly surprising that it was becoming outclassed by the opposition by the middle twenties. Thus it was superseded by the New Phantom or 'Phantom I', in 1925. Its 7668 cc., six-cylinder (in two blocks of three), pushrod overhead-valve engine put out about 100 b.h.p. The new chassis, with its cantilever rear suspension, was similar to that of the 'Silver Ghost' in most respects. In 1928 the least expensive 'Phantom I' in the Rolls-Royce catalogue was an open tourer at £2,602, and the most expensive was a cabriolet-de-ville at £2,932. Each car had a 3-year guarantee and Rolls-Royce recommended that it should be returned to them for dismantling every 50,000 miles. The 1925 example illustrated has had its Barker barrel-sided touring coachwork reconstructed in the workshops at Beaulieu after being rescued from its last job of towing a gang mower.

Over 2,200 Phantom I chassis were built at the Derby works between 1925 and 1929, when it was replaced by the 'Phantom II', while a further 1,240 were constructed at the Springfield, Massachusetts, U.S.A. factory between 1926 and 1931 – but many American purchasers preferred their status symbols to be built in the U.K. The confidence of the Company in the success of the new series was underlined by a part of their introductory announcement at its launching: 'After seven years of experiment and test . . . the 40/50 h.p. six-cylinder Phantom chassis emerged, and is offered to the public as the most suitable type possible for a mechanically-propelled carriage under present-day conditions' – leaving little more to be said . . . !

Photo : National Motor Museum

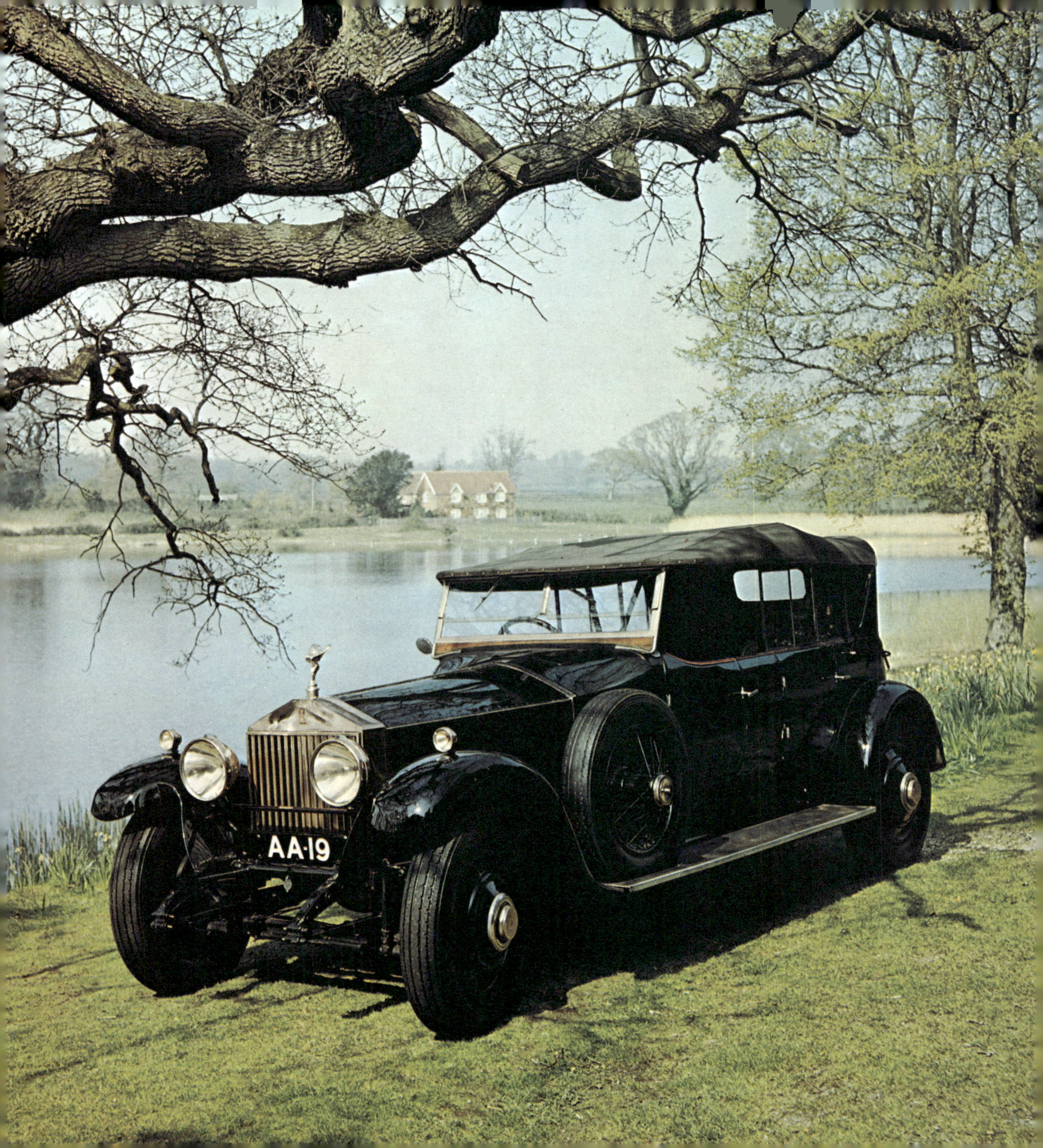
AA·19

1925 FRAZER NASH 1½-LITRE

Frazer Nash owners, who are sometimes referred to as the Chain Gang because of the unusual transmission of their cars which works by a system of chains and dog-clutches, are nearly as fiercely partisan in their allegiance to them as are the Bentley Boys and the Bugattisti to their own *marques*.

This is understandable, as the Vintage Frazer Nash, which was designed by Captain Archie Frazer-Nash, was a good sports-car indeed. Production began in 1925, and the very first cars used o.h.v. 'Powerplus' engines but these were soon changed for 1½-litre, side-valve Anzani units, which produced about 40 b.h.p. The aluminium-bodied cars were light – only 13 cwt – so 70 m.p.h. was available with the modest thirst of 40 m.p.g.

The pretty three-seater 'Super Sports' model illustrated, which belongs to the current President of the Vintage Sports Car Club, Nigel Arnold-Forster, cost about £330 in 1925.

Photo: National Motor Museum

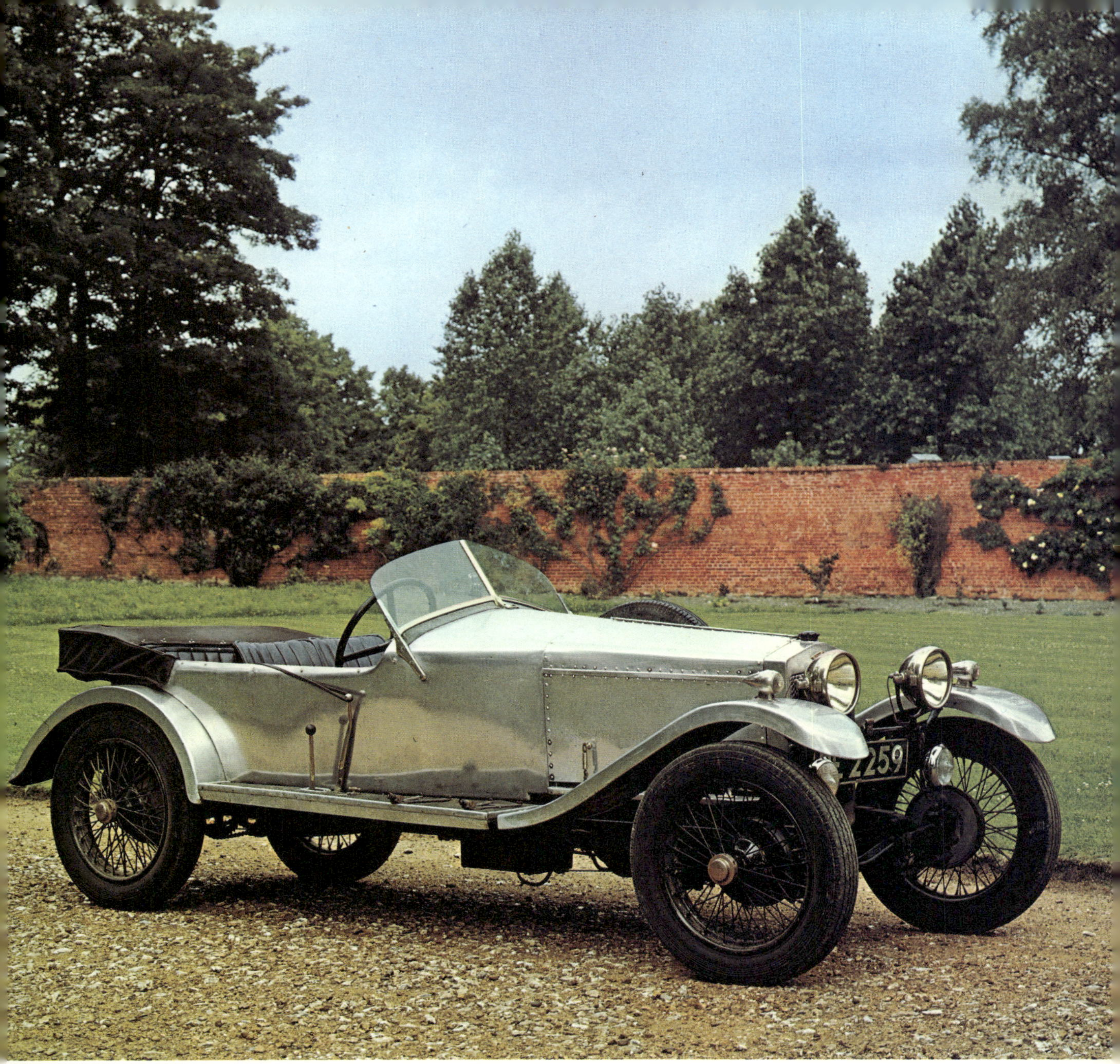
2259

1926 BENTLEY 3-LITRE SPEED MODEL

Of all the Vintage Cars, none has made a stronger or more lasting impression on the man-in-the-saloon (or the public) than W. O. Bentley's creations (see page 9).

The basic design features of all his cars are a fixed-head, four- or six-cylinder engine with four valves per cylinder and a single overhead camshaft, allied to a conventional 1920s 'bedstead' chassis of battleship proportions. Bentley reliability was a watchword and backed by a 5-year guarantee.

The original 3-litre was exhibited at the 1919 Olympia Show, but it was not available to the well-to-do sporting motorist until 1921 at £1,050 for the chassis, with body to choice as an optional extra. The enlarged version of 4½-litres came out in 1928, though it was preceded by a 6-cylinder, 6½-litre model in 1925. The deservedly-renowned, and rare, 6-cylinder 8-litre, of which but 100 examples were built between 1930 and 1932, just qualifies as a Vintage car by its 1930 introduction. It would do 100 m.p.h. with a well-appointed saloon body.

The evergreen Bentley reputation has its rock-like foundation in their memorable triumphs in *Les Vingt-quatres Heures du Mans* in the 1920s, and the Works Teams' record can bear repetition: 1923 4th (3-litre); 1924 1st (3-litre); 1927 1st (3-litre); 1928 1st and 5th (4½-litres); 1929 1st, 2nd, 3rd and 4th (6½-litre followed by three 4½-litres); 1930 1st and 2nd (6½-litres).

The Bentley Company's finances were always a little tight under the arms unfortunately, and the industrial depression of the turn of the Vintage decade, plus the withdrawal of the diamond-millionaire-cum-works-driver Woolf Barnato's financial support, resulted in a take-over by Rolls-Royce in 1931 – and a very different kind of Bentley.

Photo: London Art Tech

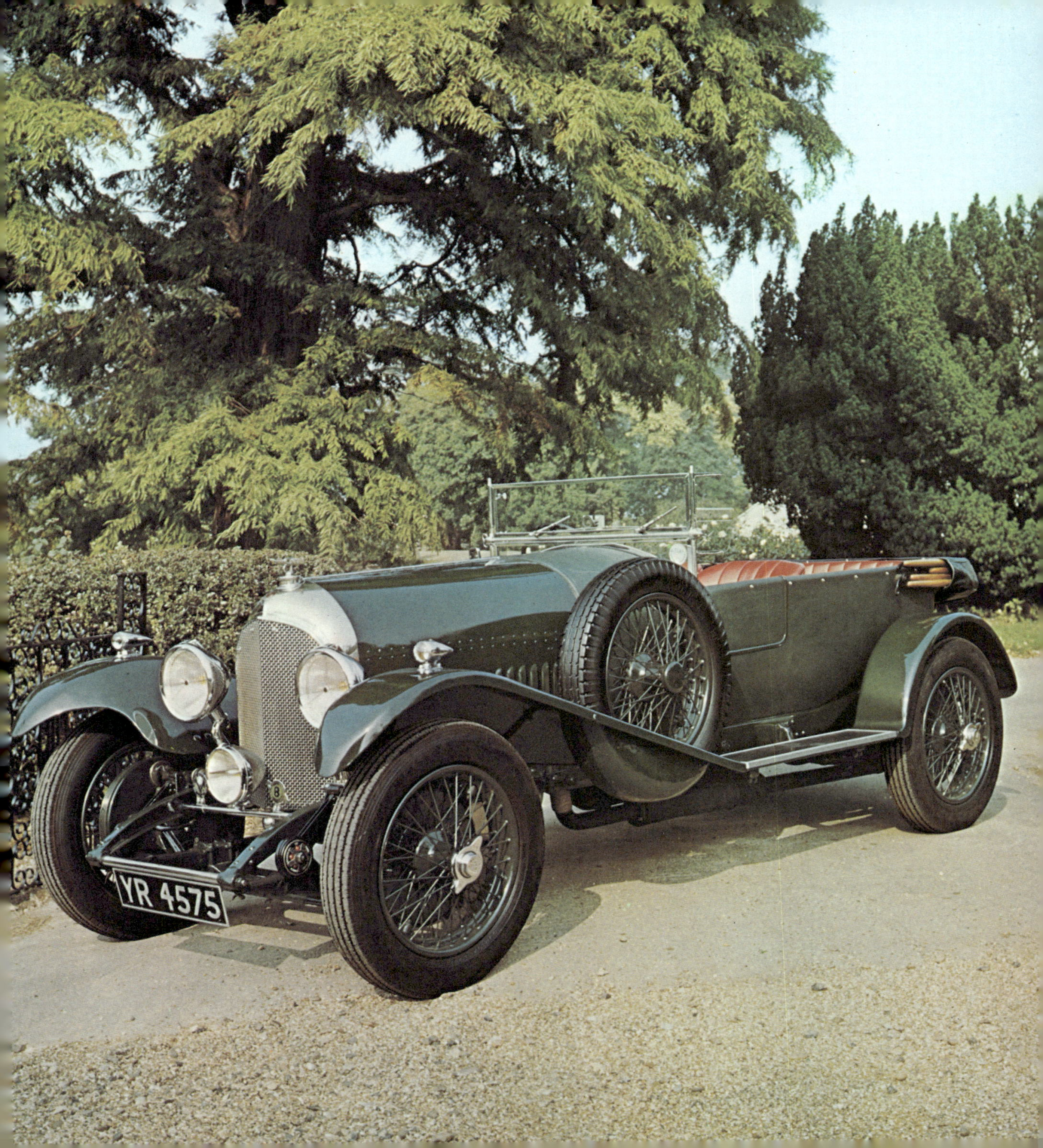
YR 4575

1926 ALVIS 12/50

The 12/50 was born in 1923 at the Alvis Car and Engineering Company, Holyhead Road, Coventry. It had a 4-cylinder, pushrod overhead-valve engine, with duralumin con-rods, of 1.5 or 1.7 litres to choice, the smaller version producing some 50 b.h.p. It was expensive for a car of its type at the time as, by the following year, a two-seater cost £550 and a four-seater a further £25. Nevertheless, you get what you pay for, and it went very well for a 1½-litre Vintage car (although it was on the heavy side) being good for over 70 m.p.h. in sports form with an excellent fuel consumption.

The 12/50 was available with several different types of body, from the elegant two-seater 'ducksback' design illustrated (which had an outside copper exhaust pipe) and the attractive 'beetleback' model, to rather mundane if worthy family tourers. It continued in production until 1932.

The works had an outstanding early victory with a 12/50 when Major C. M. Harvey won the J.C.C. 200-mile race at Brooklands in 1923 at 93 m.p.h. with a special racing version, while private owners frequently entered their cars successfully in the sprints and hill-climbs which proliferated in the Vintage years.

The delightful Vintage Alvis radiator mascot was a hare sitting up on its haunches thus, according to Peter Hull, depicting lightness allied to strength and speed. The detail pose of this hare was changed for each year of production, from its inception in 1920 to 1929/30.

Photo: London Art Tech

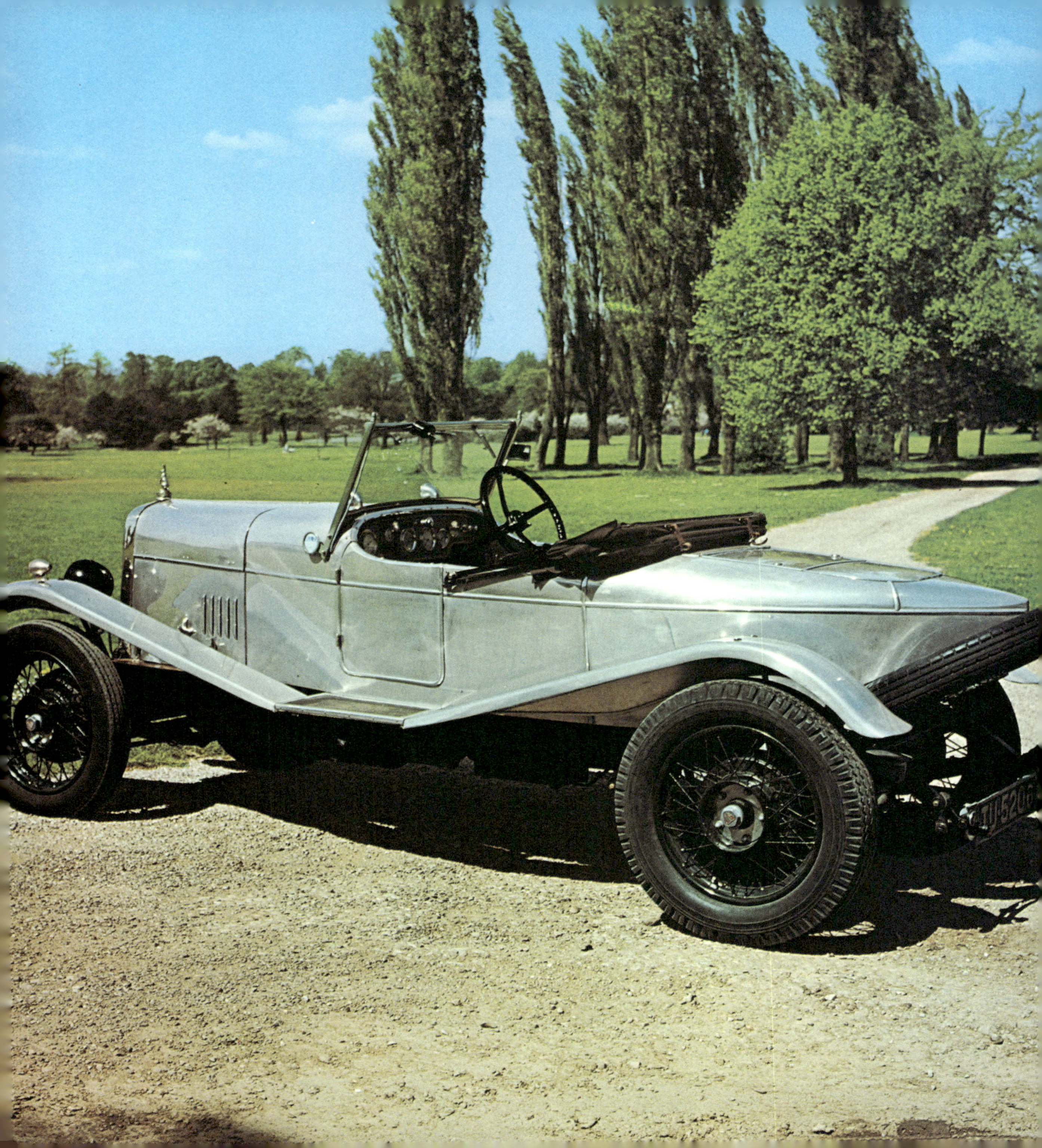

1926 SUNBEAM 3-LITRE

The début of the 3-litre Sunbeam came at *Les Vingt-quatres Heures du Mans* of 1925, when two cars were entered by the Company for Chassagne/Davis and Segrave/Duller. The latter pair led the race for a while, but they had to retire around midnight with clutch bothers, leaving the other car to last the distance – in spite of a cracked chassis – and come second to the winning Lorraine, some 45 miles astern and 1.8 m.p.h. slower overall.

This fine Vintage sporting car was aimed at the 3-litre Bentley market, which car it could out-perform. Its 6-cylinder, twin-overhead-camshaft, fixed-head engine (75 × 110 mm), with two carburettors, produced 90 b.h.p. at 3,800 r.p.m. – and 90 m.p.h. in good tune. It was an up-dated version of Bertarione's earlier racing engines.

However, the very long chassis (10 ft 10 in wheelbase), and narrow track, allied to rear cantilever springs, were the weak points of the design from a competition point of view (*vide* 1925 Le Mans above), though they behaved well enough in normal road usage. Nevertheless the 3-litre Bentley was sufficiently well-established and appreciated for the Sunbeam never to receive the sales success it deserved for its advanced features for the day, though its production survived the Vintage years. A supercharged version which gave 138 b.h.p. appeared in 1928, but very few were made.

Most of the 3-litre Sunbeams had the attractive four-seater open coachwork illustrated, but some were fitted with Weymann saloon bodies.

Photo: National Motor Museum

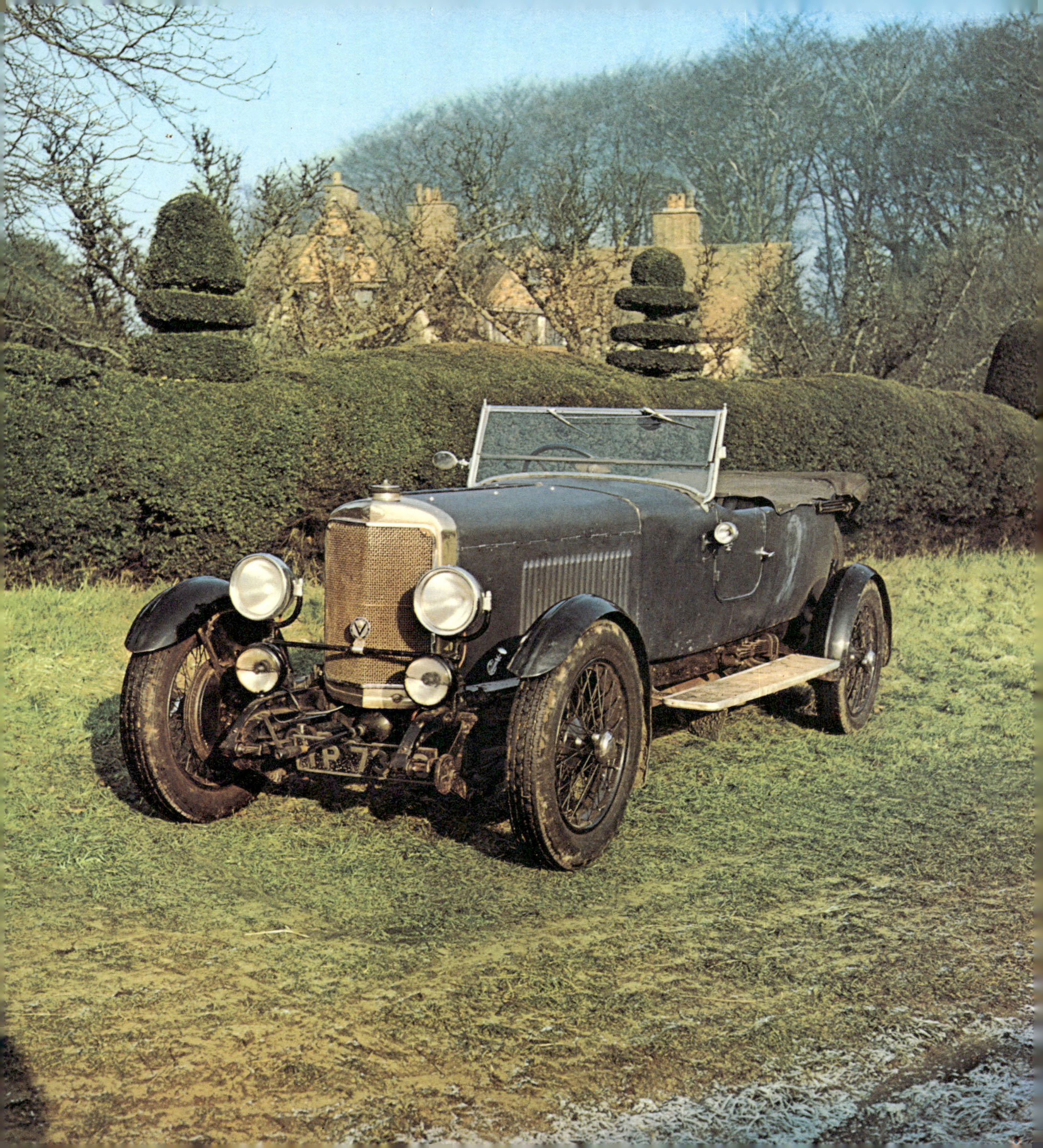

1927 JOWETT 'LONG FOUR'

Jowett Cars Limited, of Bradford, Yorkshire, established a record production run of 42 years. Their horizontally-opposed, twin-cylinder, water-cooled engine was put into their first car in 1910 and a development of it was still used in their efficient Bradford van until 1952 when the 'Javelin' appeared.

In 1922 Jowett brought out a 4-seater car, which may not have held much appeal to the connoisseur as it was of plebian appearance and finish, but with its much-advertised 'little engine with the big pull' of only 907 ccs. and a three-speed gearbox, it provided very reliable motoring at the cheaper end of the market.

The 'Long Four' tourer illustrated cost but £245 and, with its short bonnet and long body, it supplied Mr Quiverful and his bulls-eyes with economical transportation within the 7 h.p. Road Tax bracket.

Photo: National Motor Museum

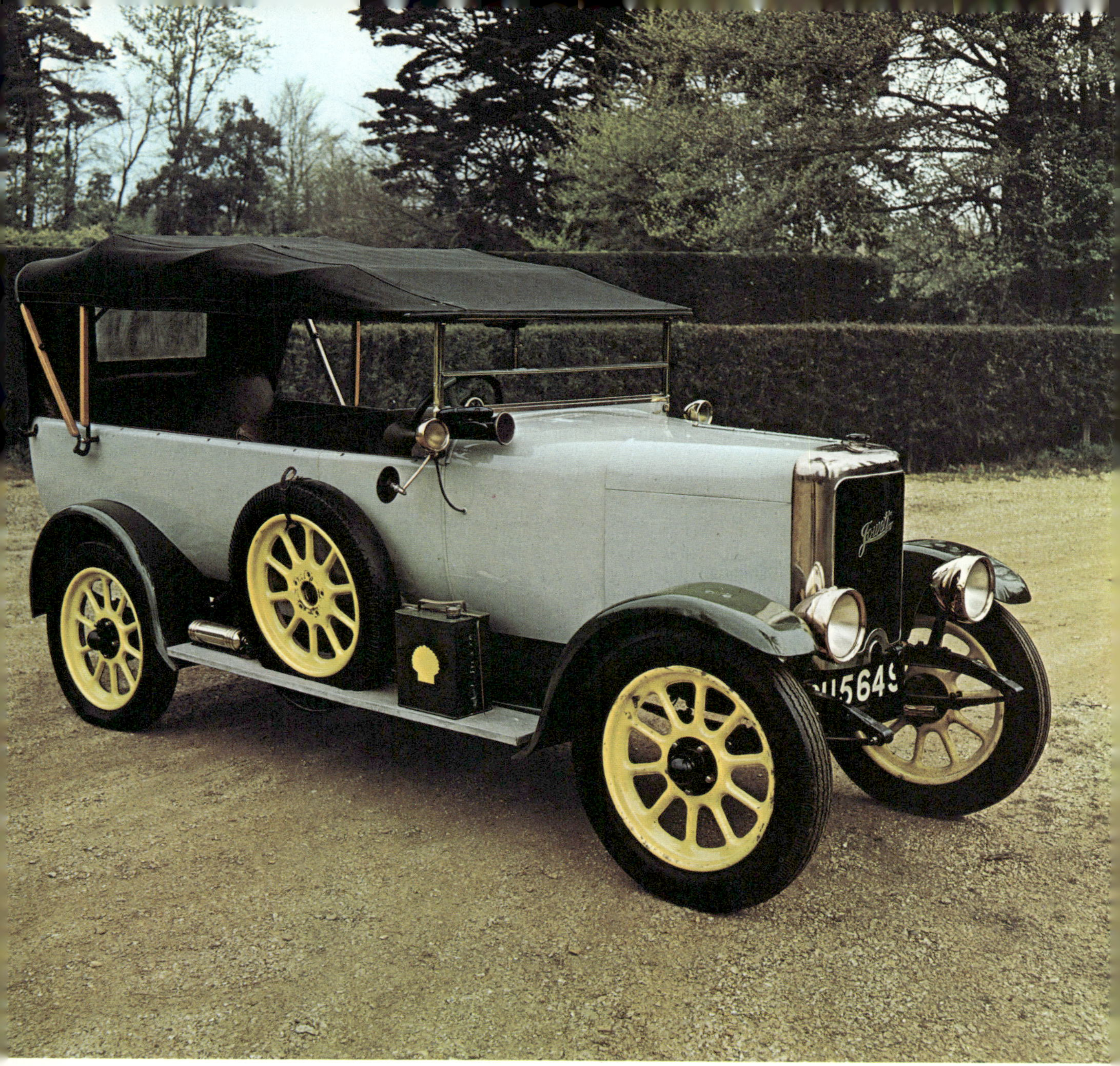

1927 ISOTTA FRASCHINI TIPO 8A

Isotta Fraschini is among the older names in the motor industry, as the Company was founded in 1899. They were pioneers of braking on all four wheels, which system they adopted in 1910, while they were also among the first serious devotees of the straight-eight engine after the war.

Like Birkigt and Bentley, Giustino Cattaneo designed aircraft engines in the 1914–18 war, and the Isotta Fraschini 6-litre pushrod o.h.v., straight-eight motor-car engine just after it. Unlike its Hispano and Bentley rivals, however, the Tipo 8 Isotta was cumbersome and heavy in its chassis, and also down on engine output compared with contemporary high-priced cars of similar capacity (see page 10). Nevertheless its manner-of-going was very refined and flexible and its appearance was extremely impressive – which was what counted with such owners as Rudolf Valentino, Clara Bow and Jack Dempsey in the U.S.A., who wanted a very large imported car of great presence, which the Tipo 8 certainly had. The chassis price in 1922 was $6,500.

A development known as the Tipo 8A, with the capacity increased to 7,372 cc., came at the end of 1924. It had distinctly improved performance and a big swallow of the order of 12 m.p.g. – not that this worried the owner of an example bodied by Castagna, with silver and ivory fittings, for which he paid 8,000 1920s £s. The Tipo 8A was the current model to the end of the Vintage period, being replaced by the Tipo 8B, on the same theme, in 1931. Peter Hampton's lovely 8A tourer has coachwork by Sala of Milan.

Photo: Charles Pocklington

YF 3270

1928 BUGATTI TYPE 44

Ettore Bugatti (1881–1947), was a great individualist to the point of mild eccentricity. Thus it is not surprising that his cars bear the unmistakable stamp of his personality; all his designs being of great, and similar, character and frequently of aesthetic beauty, as befits the work of a man who trained as an artist.

Bugatti, who designed and built his own cars as a manufacturer, was responsible for the superlative luxury car of the Vintage period – the Type 41 'Royale' (see page 10) – and one of its most successful racing cars in the Type 35 in its several versions. He also made a number of touring models, of which the Type 44 is probably the best.

The car was introduced in 1927. It had a straight-eight, o.h.c. engine of 3 litres, with 3 valves per cylinder and of great refinement, in a chassis with semi-elliptic springs at the front and reversed quarter-elliptics aft. It had a maximum speed of around 90 m.p.h. depending on the coachwork fitted, which was praiseworthy at the time for a car of its capacity.

The four-seater tourer illustrated was the property of the great American motoring writer, the late Ken W. Purdey.

Photo: National Motor Museum

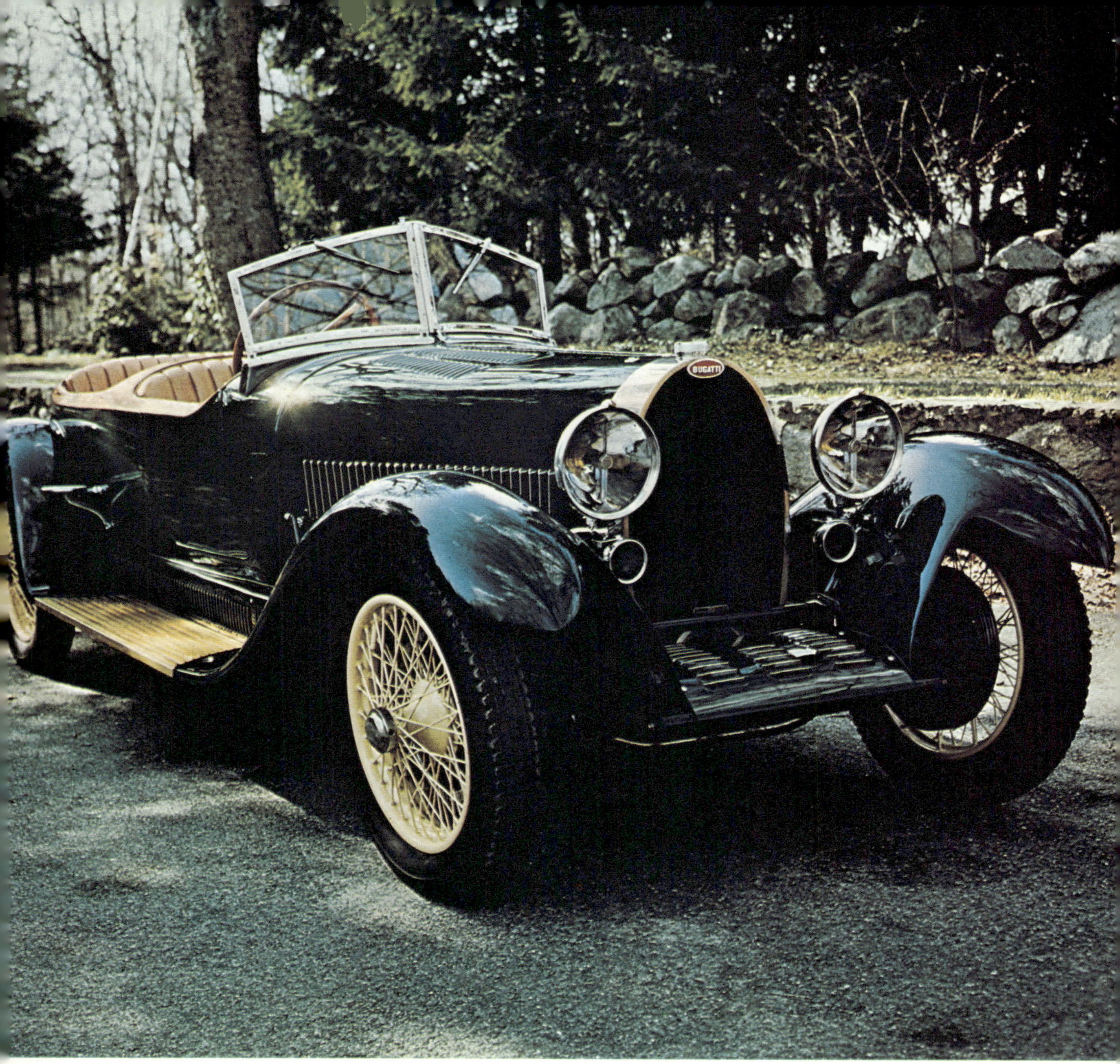
BUGATTI

1928–29 ALFA ROMEO 6C 1500

The first Mille Miglia was run on 26/27 March 1927, but Vittorio Jano's beautiful twin o.h.c., six-cylinder 1½-litre cars were not yet ready for competition work and the race was won by O.M., who took the first three places, beating two works-entered RLSS 22/90 Alfa Romeos and three private owners in similar cars. Nevertheless, as soon as they were in production in mid-1927, the 6C 1500s had immediate success, including a victory in the Circuit of Modena race with Enzo Ferrari himself at the wheel. In 1928 these supercharged 1500 cc. cars' successes included the Targa Florio (Campari) and the Mille Miglia (Campari/Ramponi), while the example illustrated provided one-half of Ivanowski's 1929 Irish Grand Prix win and a blown 17/50 the other.

The 1500 came in three versions:

15/60 h.p.: single-overhead-camshaft
15/75 h.p.: twin-overhead-camshaft 'Gran Turismo'
15/85 h.p.: twin-overhead-camshaft, supercharged, 'Super Sport'

The charming two-seater shown here is one of the latter masterpieces. The 1487 cc., six-cylinder engine (62 × 82 mm) produced 76 b.h.p. at 4,800 r.p.m. with excellent reliability, and the car was good for over 90 m.p.h. The overall design and engineering craftsmanship of these models were of the highest order, the sculptured beauty of the castings of the ribbed supercharger casing, and of the manifolds, being particularly admirable.

These great 1½-litre sports-cars were followed, in 1929, by similar cars with slightly bigger engines (65 × 88 mm) and a capacity of 1752 cc. These were known as 17/50s and made a great reputation for themselves.

Photo: National Motor Museum

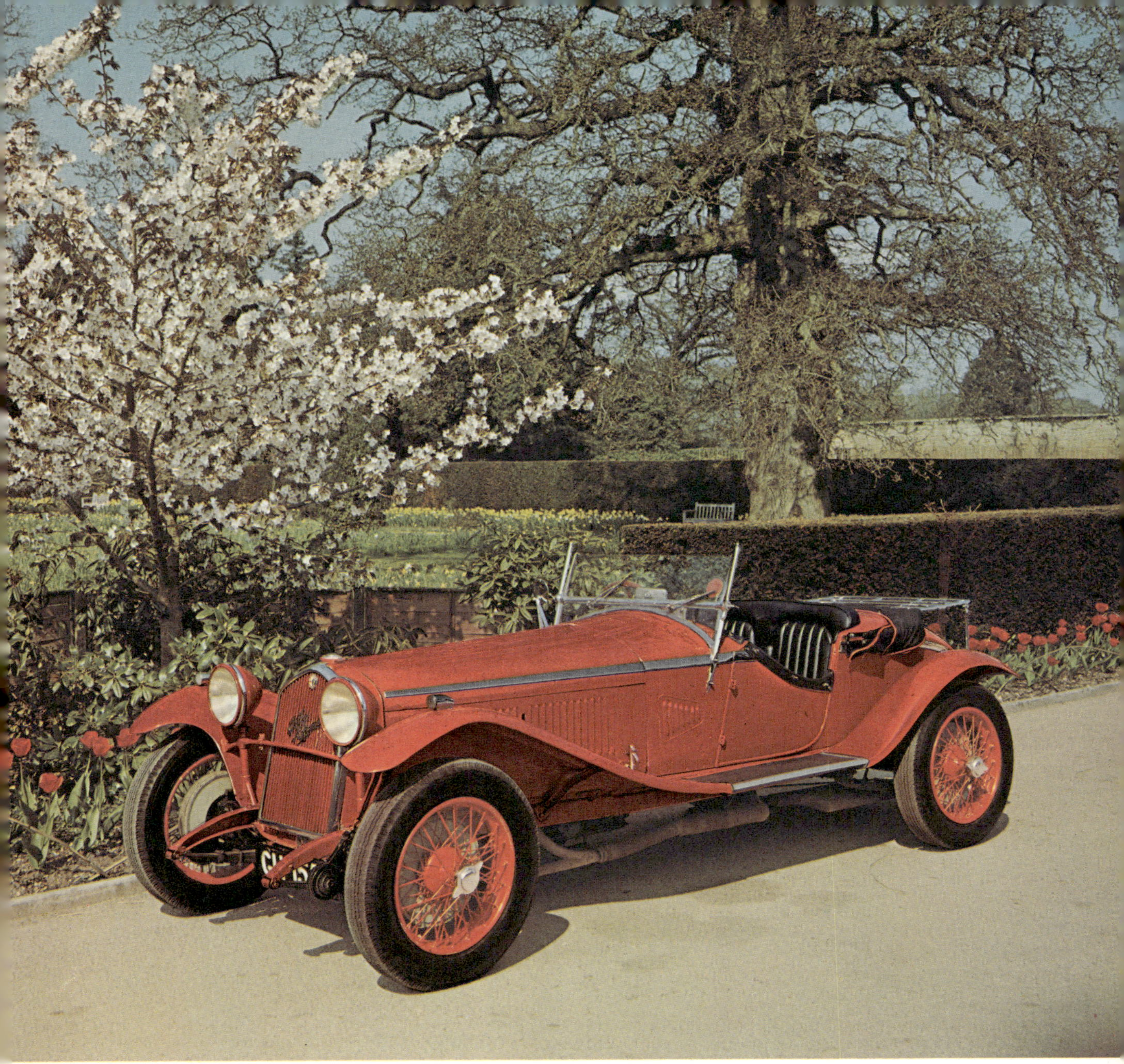

1928 LANCIA LAMBDA (Eighth Series)

That discerning Vintage *aficionado*, Bunny Tubbs, has firmly stated in print that 'the Lancia Lambda is one of the greatest Vintage cars. More than that it is one of the great cars of all time.'

Why this enthusiasm for a far-from-pretty, rather slab-sided, square-rigged-looking Italian touring car? Because this Vincenzo Lancia design was many years ahead of its time in that, when it was first put into production, it had an integral chassis, independent front suspension by vertical coil springs and a narrow V-4 o.h.c. engine of 2-litres capacity – and all this in 1922!

The Lambda came in nine Series, numbered roughly annually between 1923 and 1931, during which time the bore was increased in the 7th Series (1927/8) raising the capacity to 2.3-litres and again in the 8th (1928/31) to 2.5 litres. They were not really designed to be sports-cars, but nevertheless they were a match for, and were frequently able to see off, many contemporary so-called sports-cars of similar capacity, particularly over tortuous going, by virtue of the first-rate road-holding provided by their sliding-pillar front suspension and ultra-precise steering.

Photo: National Motor Museum

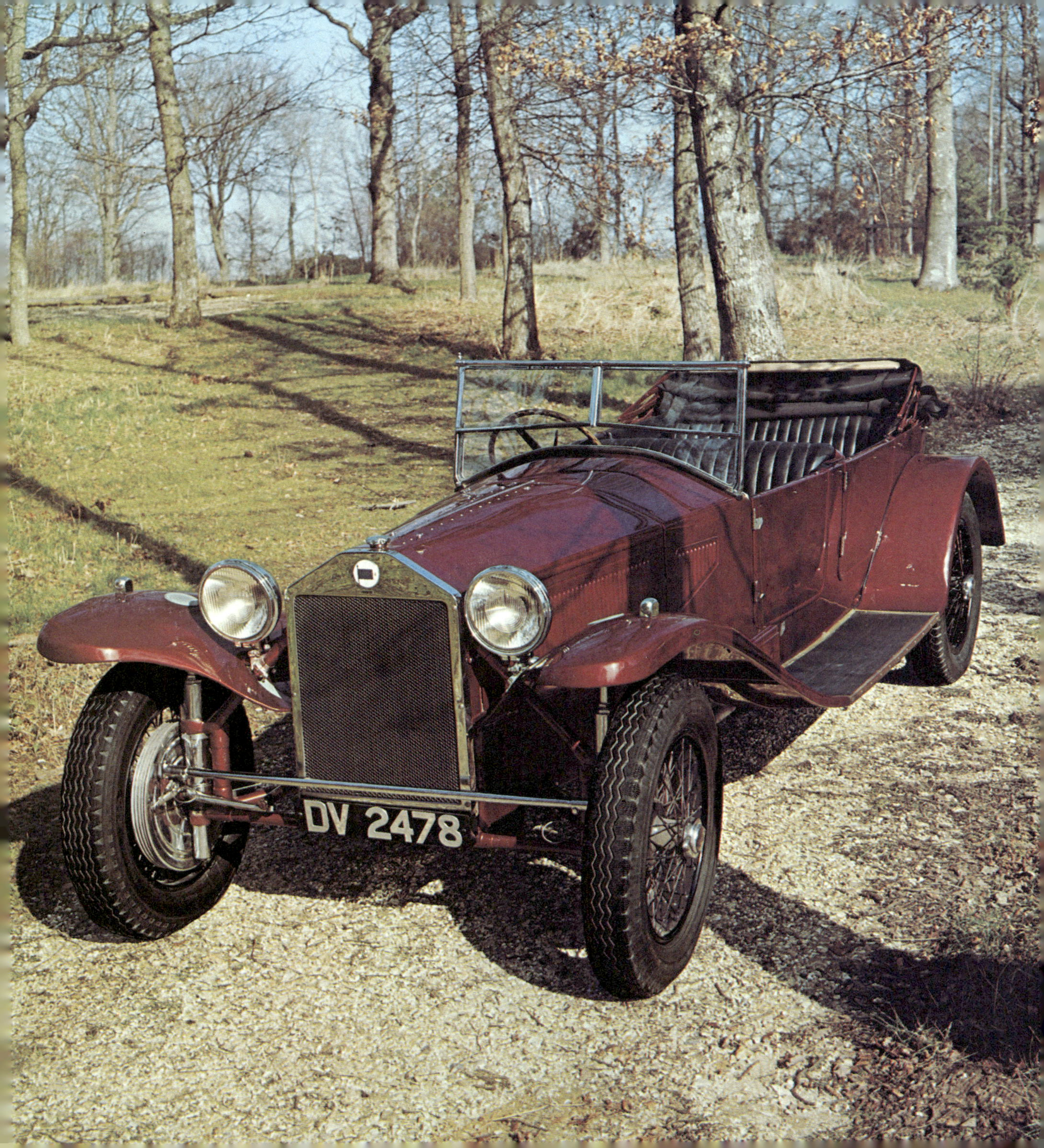
DV 2478

1929 38/250 MERCEDES-BENZ SSK

The fabulous S-type 'big six' Mercedes-Benz sports-cars of the Vintage period are the work of the great Bohemian designer, Dr Ferdinand Porsche, who was probably the most brilliant man in all the various fields of automobile design who has ever lived – his talents ranged from Grand Prix cars to the Volkswagen, from aero-engines to tanks.

The ancestor of the S-series of sports and sports-racing cars was the 33/180 model of 1927, which in turn was a supercharged version of the 33/140 of 1925. The legendary S-types were born in the great shape of the 36/220 car which appeared in 1928. It had a six-cylinder, overhead-camshaft engine of 6.789 litres, acceleration being augmented by a Roots-type supercharger blowing air through the carburettor when the throttle-pedal was depressed beyond its normal travel, thus engaging a friction clutch. A most satisfying banshee-wail, plus an impressive shove in the back, resulted! But you weren't supposed to keep it engaged for long.... The 36/220 was followed in 1929 by the even larger 38/250 (7.069 litres) which produced 160 b.h.p., and 200 b.h.p. with the blower in action. There were three types of chassis: SS (normal), SSK (short chassis) and SSKL [Super Sport *kurz* (short) *leicht* (light)] though the latter were usually 'works' sports-racing cars and very few were sold.

These cars were reasonably light in weight for their great size and they were superbly engineered, while a very high top gear ratio provided effortless fast cruising at low engine r.p.m. They had some splendid racing successes, especially in the hands of the top Mercedes-Benz 'works' driver, Rudolf Caracciola.

Photo: London Art Tech

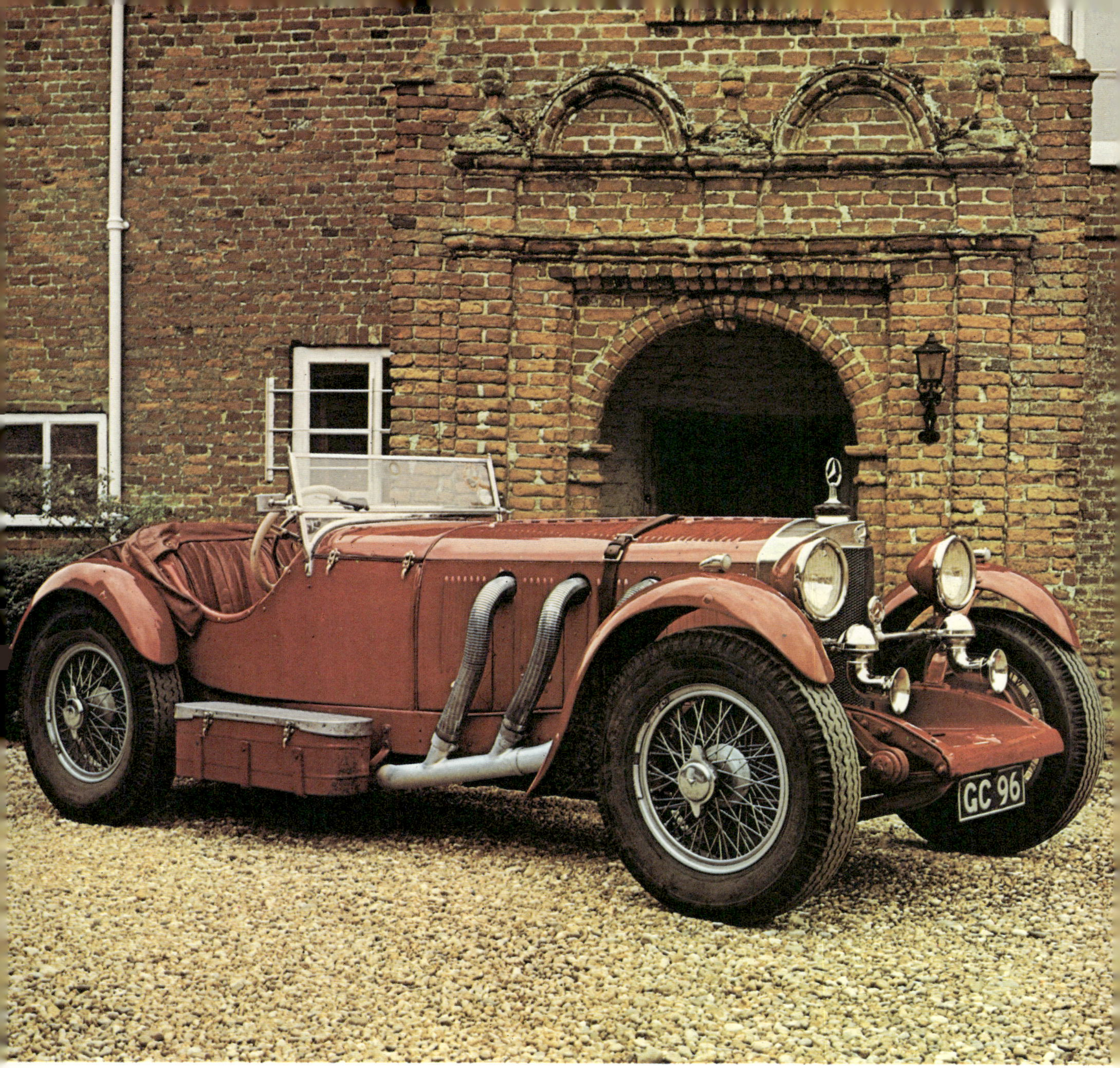
GC 96

1929 DUESENBERG MODEL J

In their works at Indianapolis, Indiana, U.S.A., Frederick and August Duesenberg designed and built the outstanding American car of the Vintage period (see page 10).

In 1926 E. L. Cord (of Auburn) had gained control of the Company, which had been building its excellent 4.2-litre Model A (and the very similar Model X) since 1920. Cord insisted that the replacement must be a truly exceptional luxury high-performance car – which the Model J undoubtedly turned out to be. Its 7-litre straight-eight engine was credited with producing 265 b.h.p., which made 89 m.p.h. available in second gear and, in top, the Model J was good for close on 120 m.p.h. As if this was not good enough, the Brethren shortly produced a supercharged version, known as the SJ, which had a top gear range of 31 to 130 m.p.h., and delivered 320 b.h.p., but it came just outside the Vintage period – in 1932.

A Duesenberg chassis cost around $8,500, and with a body by one of the best American coachbuilders – like Le Baron (who built that on the car opposite), or Rollston – the total bill could be well nigh $18,000 (£4,500), which was a lot of money to pay for a motor-car in 1929.

Photo: George A. Moffit

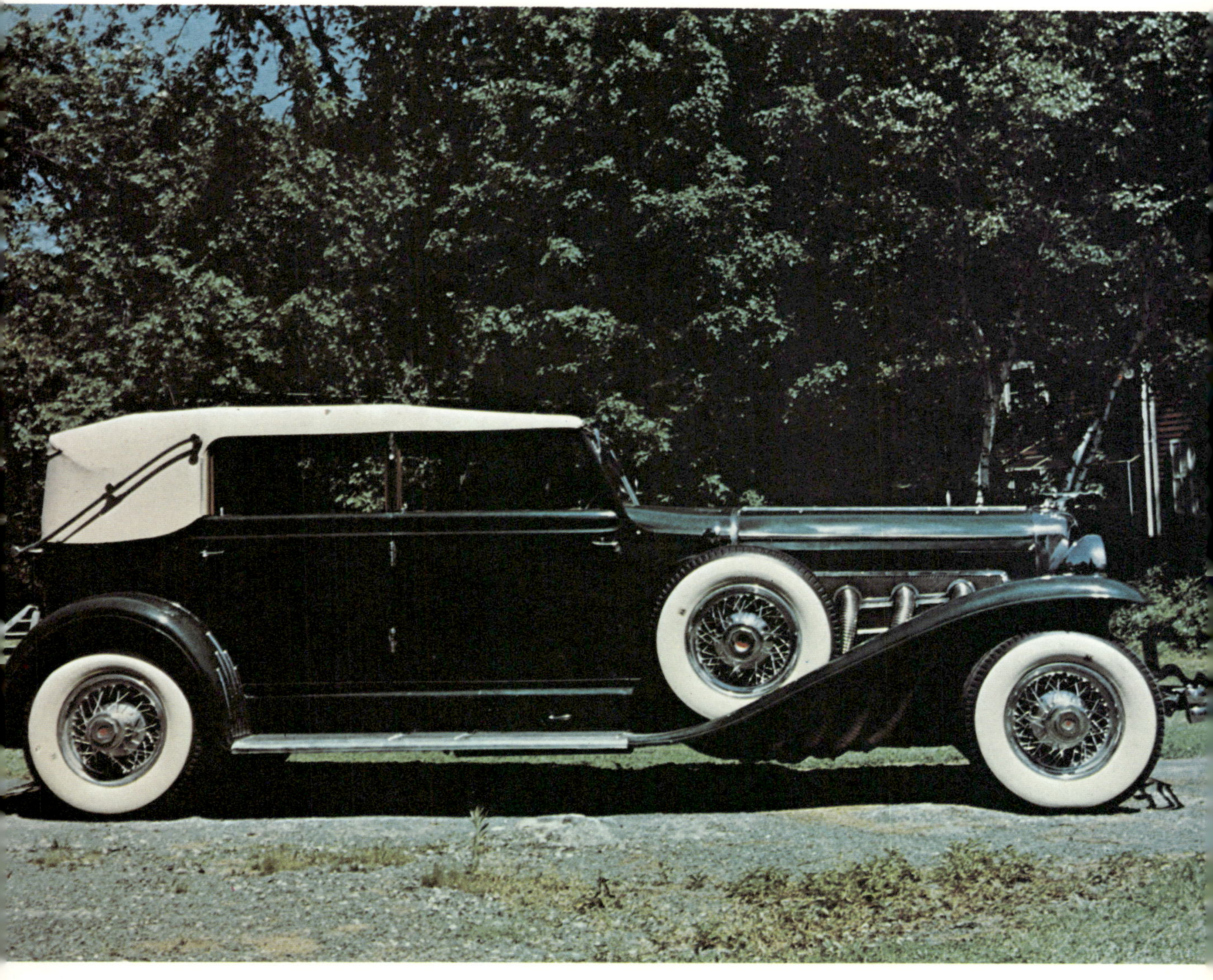

1929 IRVING-NAPIER 'GOLDEN ARROW'

On 11 March 1929, the World Land Speed Record was raised by nearly 24 m.p.h. by the Irving-Napier driven by Major H. O. D. Segrave.

This very striking and efficient car was designed by J. S. Irving (previously of Sunbeam) around a 23.9-litre Napier aero-engine, with its 12 cylinders in W-formation, of the type used in the Supermarine seaplanes which won the Schneider Trophy. It gave 925 b.h.p. at 3,300 r.p.m., and drove the rear wheels, through a three-speed gearbox, by two separate propeller shafts with the driver sitting between them to keep him as low as possible. The sponsons between the faired front and rear wheels housed aircraft-type surface radiators, and the wheelbase was 14 feet. The beautifully streamlined body was made in aluminium, and finished in gold, by Thrupp and Maberly, and the car was built at the K.L.G. sparking plug factory at Putney Vale at the expense of wealthy sponsors.

The record attempt at Daytona Beach, Florida went very well. After a two-way practice run at about 180 m.p.h., which was followed by a 14-day delay for bad weather, Segrave and the 'Golden Arrow' flew through the measured mile in 15.55 secs. in one direction and in 15.57 secs. on the return run – an average speed of 231.446 m.p.h. This comfortably beat Ray Keech's 1928 record of 207.552. On his return to England, Major Segrave was knighted for this, and his many other achievements.

The 'Golden Arrow' was presented by Castrol to the National Motor Museum in 1971.

Photo: National Motor Museum

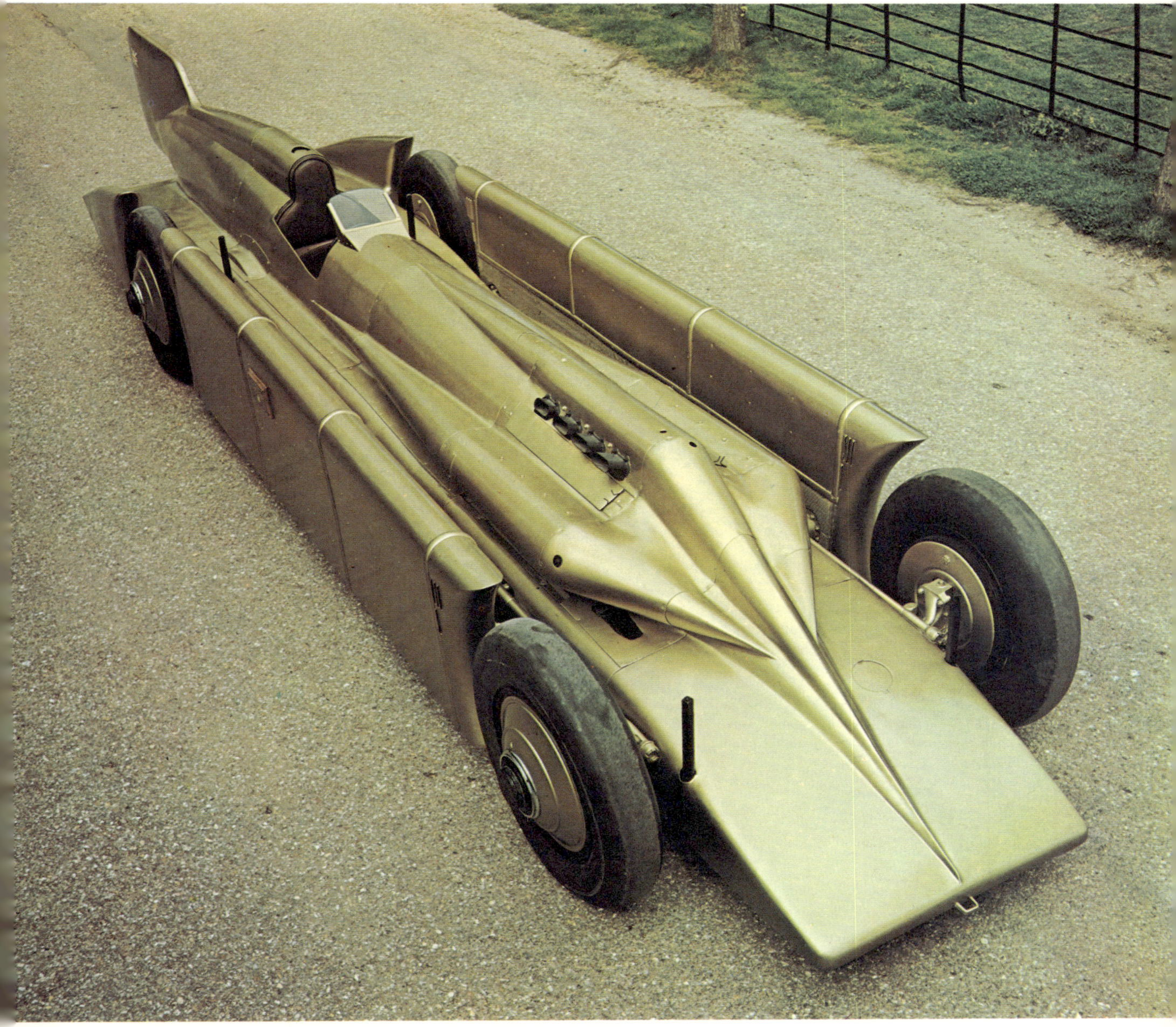

1930 M.G. 18/80 MARK II

The *marque* M.G. is so closely associated today with small, frenetic machinery that the earlier, more dignified, Cecil Kimber products tend to get overlooked.

M.G.'s first six-cylinder model, announced in 1928, used a fairly advanced 2½-litre o.h.c. engine in a light, but rather frail, chassis whose transmission and brakes owed much to William Morris – too much, perhaps, for a car capable of nearly 80 m.p.h. . . . So the Mark II version was beefed-up somewhat with a heavier chassis frame, stronger axles of wider track, greatly improved brakes and a four-speed gearbox featuring M.G.'s first remote-control lever. As the first complete chassis to be conceived specifically as an M.G., it was given an 'A' prefix to the range of chassis numbers, and its announcement coincided with the Company's move from Oxford to their famous Abingdon-on-Thames factory in late 1929.

Very much a Vintage car in conception, the M.G. 18/80 survived well into the post-Vintage era, production ending in mid-1933. The example shown is one of 14 produced with an aluminium two-seater body by Carbodies of Coventry, and one of four known survivors. It carried a price-tag of £625 in 1930 but was bought for £5 some 30 years later and restored to splendid and original condition by the M.G. pundit, F. Wilson McComb, whose book *The Story of the M.G. Sports Car*, is the standard work on the make.

Photo: Eric Adkins

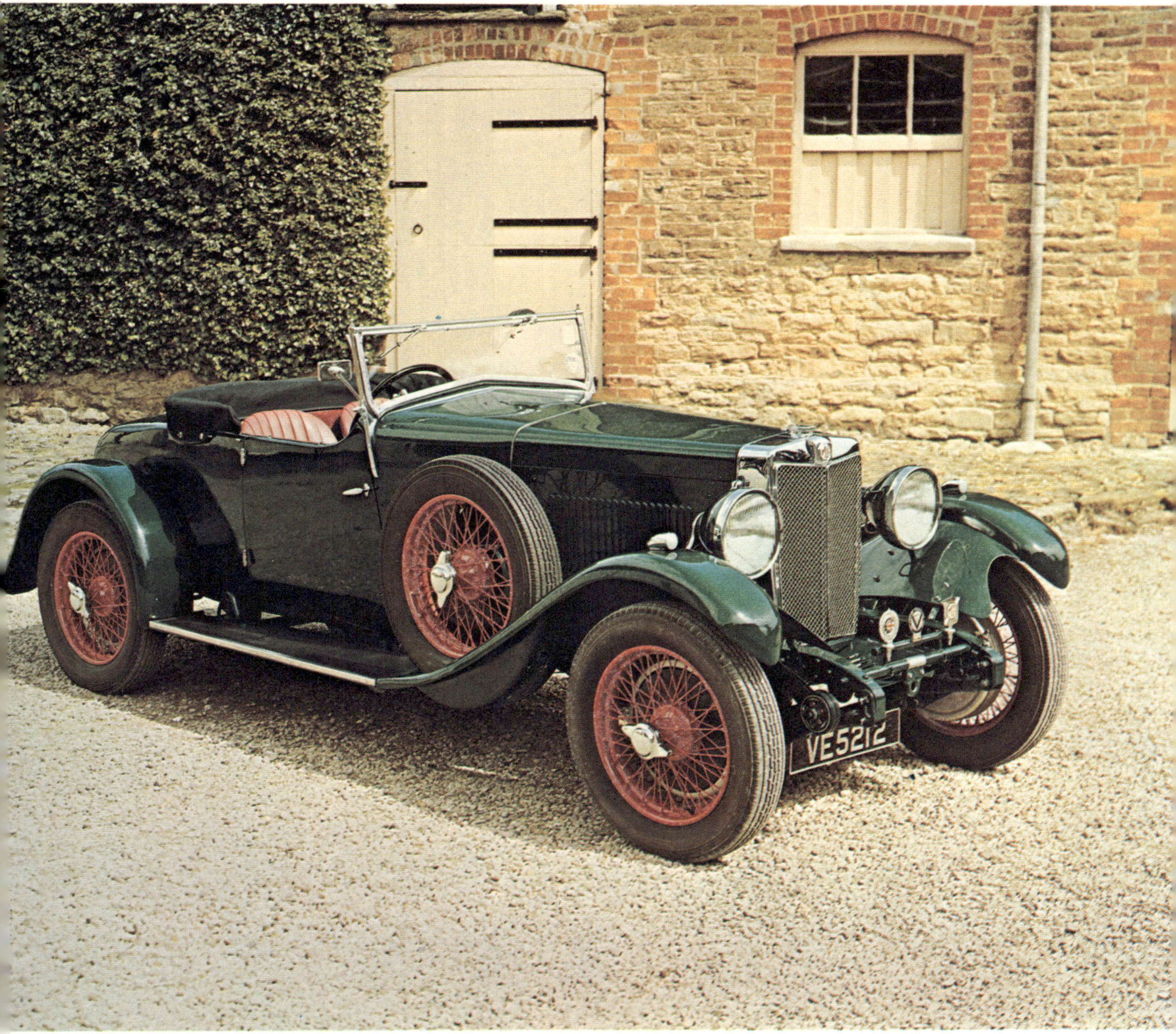
VE5212